This book is dedicated to—

My husband Patrick, whose encouragement
keeps me at my keyboard...

My present furry companions, who can
often be found *on* my keyboard...

And all the beloved pets (yours and mine)
that have brought us so much joy.

A Poem for the Grieving...

Do not stand at my grave and weep.
I am not there, I do not sleep.
I am a thousand winds that blow,
I am the diamond glints on snow.
I am the sunlight on ripened grain,
I am the gentle autumn's rain.
When you awaken in the morning's hush,
I am the swift uplifting rush
of quiet birds in circled flight.
I am the stars that shine at night.
Do not stand at my grave and cry,
I am not there, I did not die...

—*Anonymous*

Contents

Beware the Leash

It appears quite harmless
On the pet shop wall.
It's just a training tool
To teach, protect, that's all.

One end is for your friend,
One end you will hold.
It easily unattaches
Or so you have been told.

But what about the perfect fit
Molded by good times shared?
A bond has subtly grown
Because two hearts have cared.

It's no longer leather,
It seeks no restraining.
A ribbon of love has formed
Attachment unending.

Too soon the heartstring sags,
Leather reclaims the wall.
Numbly your grasp searches;
One end is filled—that's all.

Beware the leash, my friends.
Its powers are great indeed.
For if it ties your hearts,
They will know eternity.

—*Shannon and Maureen Andrews*

Foreword

In my 17 years of psychotherapy practice, I have counseled many people who were grieving over the loss of a pet. I know how devastating it can be for someone to face the death of their cherished animal friend. But until now, I was unable to recommend a book that could help.

At long last, a book has been written to help us cope with the loss of this beloved family member, the family pet. Moira Anderson understands how painful and lonely the death of a pet can be. She has written a compassionate, practical, and comprehensive guide to help us deal successfully with the loss of a beloved companion.

Anderson's book intelligently and sensitively discusses all aspects of pet grief. Her book is carefully crafted and treats this serious subject with wisdom and candor. Her suggestions are sensible, and allow the reader to deal openly with a grieving process that is all too often kept hidden because the reader was embarrassed or afraid no one would understand. She sheds a welcome ray of light on a subject that has far too long been underestimated, misunderstood and ignored.

The reality is that millions of Americans own, and have developed deep and meaningful attachments with, pets of all kinds. When such a pet dies or must be euthanized, the owner has few resources to help him or her understand and cope with the grief that follows. Yet if this grieving process remains hidden and is not worked through, too often it can result in other psychological and health problems for the individual. Anderson has created a very helpful book filled with information and guidance to meet the needs of such a grieving owner.

This book should be required reading for anyone who brings a pet into the family. It is a first-rate book that is overdue and well done. It should also be a valuable tool to any professional who will be called upon to help someone deal with the death of a family pet.

—Dr. Diane Kelley
Manhattan Beach, CA
September 1987

Introduction

MY HUSBAND AND I were watching television and weren't paying attention to the time. Only when the movie ended did we realize that it was after 11 pm, and Sebell, our black cat, had not yet asked to come in. Usually he would have been scratching at the door long before then, and would have stuffed himself full of kibble, kicked his sister off the couch, and settled down for an evening nap. But not that night.

We called; no cat. We wandered up and down the street, calling; have you any idea how difficult it is to search for a black cat at night? Our neighbor poked his head out the window to talk to us, and as we walked up the driveway to converse in more normal tones, we found Sebell.

We'll never know who laid him so carefully in the neighbor's driveway. Perhaps it was the driver of the car that struck him. Perhaps it was a passerby who found him in the street. Perhaps someone saw him race out of that driveway (next to our own) and assumed that this was where he lived. His body was already stiff and cold.

Though both of us had lost pets in the past, it was the first time that we had lost one as a couple, the first time we had lost a member of our new family unit. And that was exactly how we felt, as we wept and grieved together that night: that a member of our family had died.

One can't put one's misery aside and trot off calmly to work the next morning as if nothing had happened. At the time, however, I had a job that anyone in my position would surely have envied. I was the editor of *Dog Fancy* magazine, and instead of being surrounded by insensitive coworkers who might not have understood my red eyes and sniffling, I was surrounded by pet lovers. All my fellow editors had households full of birds, dogs, cats, and even horses, and they fully understood my loss. I even received a sympathy desk visit from Molly the office cat (though she may have been looking for my Egg McMuffin).

I also had a painfully appropriate task to perform: Months ago, we had decided to run a survey on dealing with pet loss. Now it was no longer an intellectual exercise; as I prepared the survey, I truly wanted to know how other pet lovers had dealt with the feelings and issues that I was facing.

Perhaps *because* this survey was written from the heart— or more likely, because it touched so closely the hearts of so many other pet lovers—it drew the greatest response of any survey we had ever run. Dozens of readers wrote that this was the first time they had ever had a chance to express their feelings on the subject. People poured out their pain, and offered sympathy and valuable advice to other readers who faced the same experience. "Just writing this letter makes me feel better," said one respondent.

The survey drew nearly 600 responses—and I was struck by a theme that kept repeating itself in letter after letter. Though the hundreds of letters described much the same elements of grief and recovery, almost every writer said the same thing: "I suppose I'm probably the only person to feel this way." Each of these respondents felt alone in their grief; many even wondered if they were crazy, if something was wrong with them for reacting so strongly to the death of a pet. Many had found no comfort from family or friends, and many had been told point blank that they were taking the death of their pet much too seriously. After all, many were told, it was "just an animal," and "you can always get another one."

Somebody, I thought, needs to tell these people—and all the people like them who wouldn't have a chance to read the survey and its response—that they are *not* alone! Somebody needs to tell them that their grief is normal, that it is shared by thousands of pet owners just like them, that they are not crazy. Somebody needs to tell them not to listen to the unsympathetic neighbor who says "you can always get another one" and listen, instead, to the truth that lies within their own hearts: *pet loss hurts!*

Somewhere along the line, I got the idea that "somebody" could be me. And that was how, five years ago, *Coping with Sorrow on the Loss of Your Pet* was born.

The book didn't happen instantly or overnight, and it wasn't easy. I had written plenty of articles, but a whole book? Yet in many ways this book almost wrote itself, because I didn't have to do it alone.

People like you wrote it with me.

Coping with Sorrow isn't just one person's perspective on pet loss, one person's advice. It is the shared experience of pet owners like yourself, from all over the country. More than 75 pet owners agreed to share their feelings, insights, suggestions, and advice about what worked for them. They speak to you as the friends you may have wished you had when your pet died, a friend who could speak to you with sympathy and understanding, and help guide you through the stages of grief. The pet owners quoted in this book know that not everyone understands what it means to lose a pet, and how lonely you can feel in this time of loss. This is their way of "being there" for you.

This book is dedicated to the pets of all those wonderful people who shared their grief with me—to Cammie and Sam and Hurky, to Titsie and Jasper and Trina, and to the pets whose names don't appear on these pages but whose memories live on in the hearts of their owners. It is dedicated to Sebell, and the memories of the many dogs and cats who have brightened my life. And finally, it is dedicated to those pets whom we have yet to meet, those memories we have yet to discover. I hope this book will make those meetings sweeter and the partings easier as we come to understand more clearly just how much our pets mean in our lives.

And Now, a Word About Our Second Edition...

When I set out to revise *Coping with Sorrow on the Loss of Your Pet*, I had grand plans for sweeping revisions and great changes. Fortunately, a wise old adage came to mind: If it ain't broke, don't fix it!

Based on the warm letters I've received since the first edition of *Coping with Sorrow* came out, the book "ain't broke." It didn't need fixing. But it did need a few minor revisions, some updates, and a new chapter: Chapter 10, "Giving Up a Pet." The appendix has been updated and shortened; for example, there are now so many more pet loss bereavement counselors in the country than when this book first came out that it would be impossible to list them all. Instead, I have listed resources to help you locate a counselor should you want one. I've also added a some new comments and suggestions from several bereavement counselors with whom I've spoken since the first edition came out.

I still welcome your letters and comments, and do make an effort to answer them (especially if a stamped, self-addressed envelope is included). Let me know if there's something you want to see included in the Third Edition, should that ever come to be! In the meantime, I hope and pray that *Coping with Sorrow on the Loss of Your Pet* helps you through the most difficult time a pet owner must face.

—Moira Anderson Allen, M.Ed.
Los Angeles, CA
April 1994

Chapter 1

Understanding
Your Loss

F EW THINGS IN LIFE CUT SO DEEP or leave so painful a wound as the loss of a loved one. To many people,
the term "loved one" means a human companion—a
spouse, a child, a parent, a sibling. If you are a pet owner,
however, you know the term has a much broader meaning. A
loved one may be the dog who stood by you through the most
difficult times of your life, the cat that was the child you never
had, the horse that carried you from awkward adolescence to
adulthood, or any of a host of other animal companions. When
you love pets, you know that a loved one can be any being
that shares your life and your heart, and that love knows no
species boundaries.

Like everyone else, pet owners are often ill-prepared to
face the loss of a loved one. If you have lost a pet for the first
time, you may have been completely unprepared for the range
and intensity of emotions you experienced. Even if you have
lived through many pets and know what feelings you can expect when one dies, you may be at the mercy of those feelings,
with no guidelines to help you cope. Grief is like a swamp;
without a map, it's easy to lose any sense of where you are
going or where you have been. Once lost, the more you flail

about trying to fight through the morass, the deeper you sink, and the more hopeless things look.

This book is intended to be a map to guide you through that swamp. It will show you the path that this type of grief usually takes, and outline steps you can follow to find your way back to solid ground again. If you have recently experienced, or are trying to prepare for, your first pet loss, you may not believe that solid ground is there at all, but it is. Thousands of pet owners have been over the same ground, often many times; as a pet owner who has already outlived six dogs and seven cats over the years, I'm one of them. Many other pet owners who have been there and back will also share their experiences and personal routes to recovery with you.

The first part of the recovery process involves understanding your own emotional reactions to the death of your pet. Pain, anger, grief, depression and guilt are all common reactions; these are the classic emotions associated with the loss of a human loved one, and psychologists are beginning to realize that they may be just as strong when the loss is a pet. Later we'll look at these reactions in greater detail to help you understand why they occur, how they are most likely to affect you in your specific situation, and what you can do to work through them.

The second part of the recovery process involves learning to cope with the physical absence of your pet. While a pet's death evokes the reactions described above, it is the continued absence of that pet that serves as a constant reminder of your loss, reinforcing those emotions and making them more difficult to handle. The loss of a pet creates a genuine hole in the life of a pet owner. It's not just a physical hole—the lack of a pet where you are accustomed to seeing one—but a hole in your daily schedule, the social and emotional interactions you are accustomed to, and even in your usual thought patterns. Just when you think you have your feelings under control, you look at your dog's favorite toy or your cat's bed, and the grief breaks out all over again.

Nothing can ever completely fill that hole, as nothing can ever replace a loved one, animal or human. However, there are ways to readjust your life, your thinking and your routines to make the hole less noticeable and therefore less painful. In time, as you progress through the grief-swamp to the solid ground of a "normal" emotional state again, that hole will change from a bitter gap to a well of pleasant memories.

There is no miracle cure for grief. Love is not forgotten overnight, and it is the love you feel or felt for your pet that makes its loss so devastating. Our experiences, however, may make your path smoother and make the obstacles to recovery a little easier to overcome. You will find not only specific coping strategies for your own use, but techniques to help other members of your household (including other pets) negotiate the same swamp. You'll find help in handling some of the more difficult and painful decisions you may have to make in relation to the death of your pet, such as euthanasia, and the decision of how to handle your pet's final remains.

One final word before we go on. You may find passages or anecdotes in the chapters ahead that touch a chord of familiarity in your heart, perhaps a particularly poignant reminder of your own pet or your own feelings. You may be inclined to sniffle a bit when you read such passages. One of the key factors in coping is accepting your feelings and reactions, rather than being embarrassed by them—so go ahead! A sniffle is amazingly therapeutic; don't think this author didn't experience a few herself in the course of writing this book. So grab some tissues, settle down in a comfortable chair, and when you're ready, we'll continue.

The Value of a Pet

When you lose something, your friends may often ask, "Oh, was it valuable?" By this they mean "How much did you pay for it?" or "How much could you sell it for?" That's a perfectly appropriate question if the item you lost is a piece of jewelry, say, or a family heirloom.

Unfortunately, when one loses a pet, a great many people who don't understand the pet/owner relationship may ask that same question—was it valuable? Such people can understand why you might be upset over the loss of a $500 purebred dog or grand champion cat, but if the dog was a $25 shelter mutt or the cat a bedraggled stray you took in off the street, what's the problem? Such an animal wasn't "valuable." These are the type of people who are liable to say things like "It was just an animal" or "You can always get another one."

Pet owners know, however, that the value of a pet has nothing whatsoever to do with its financial worth. Love is not based on price tags. Love, however, is in a certain sense an investment: an investment in emotions, with a virtually unlimited potential for emotional returns.

Research has shown that these returns may be higher than anyone ever imagined. A good relationship with a pet has been shown to relieve stress, lower blood pressure, help heart disease patients recover more quickly, give the elderly new purpose in life, aid the mentally handicapped relate more fully to the world around them, and much more. Pet therapy is now widely used in hospitals, nursing homes, prisons, mental facilities, facilities for the terminally ill, facilities for the physically handicapped, and many other places. Dogs, cats, birds, rabbits and horses are among the animals that have taken part in these therapeutic roles. If pets can do so much for so many, it's small wonder that they can seem to work minor miracles in our own everyday lives!

Your pet may not be a miracle therapy dog that has helped the lame walk and the elderly reach out, but you undoubtedly have your own measure of the returns it has given on your emotional investment. Companionship, confidence, sympathy, warmth—these benefits of pet ownership can't be measured in dollars, but at the same time your life would have been infinitely poorer without them.

Understanding the value of your pet in your life is an important part of understanding why its loss is so traumatic. If you listen to the "it was just a dog" statements of friends or perhaps of your own family, you may begin to wonder why your reactions to a pet's death are so severe. You may be tempted to think that, logically, this point of view is accurate: A pet is not "worth" much, you can "get another," and "it isn't as if a family member died." Why, then, are you so upset?

As Kathi W., a New York pet owner, points out, "No matter what anyone says, you have every right to take grief over the loss of a pet seriously." Why? P.M. of New Jersey says, "The relationship you have with a pet is as precious and meaningful as a relationship with a person."

These statements are reminders that, logical though the

negative comments above may seem, they are not true. Your pet was not literally human, but it may have had many "human" characteristics; and, as we'll see below, a pet can certainly earn the title of "family member." Your pet has immeasurable worth, based on its loving, emotional and perhaps spiritual contribution to your life and well-being. You cannot "get another," because nothing can replace a lost loved one. You can and probably should get a new pet (this will be discussed in greater detail in Chapter Five), but that pet should never be a replacement; instead, it will be a new loved one in its own right.

Here are some examples of the returns one can receive on an "investment" in pet ownership:

When Sue K. of Nebraska adopted her Siamese cat Titsiepritzel, he was an abused stray of indeterminate age who had already led a hard life. According to Sue, however, her own hard times were just beginning. "I had experienced a series of minor and major calamities," she wrote, "including a diagnosis of a serious chronic illness, chemical dependency, a devastating love affair and the loss of a promising career. There were times during this phase of my life when I felt that Titsie was my only friend. Once, I remember, I was lying on the couch crying, and Titsie was sitting on my chest patting my cheek with his paw and licking the tears from my face."

It is not surprising that the loss of this companion came as a devastating shock to Sue. "It was by far the most painful loss through death I have ever experienced," she wrote. "The very fact that the loss of a pet caused me more anguish than the deaths of certain elderly family members and acquaintances created some feelings of guilt and trauma, and I think that may be more typical than many people would admit."

Eleanor R. of Iowa had experienced the love and support of her dogs during hard times. "These two precious best friends had seen me through two major cancer surgeries," Eleanor wrote. "They had accepted me with one eye and half my colon removed, with no questions, no pity, only joy that I was still alive! Through my long, wakeful nights they stayed at my side; through my weeping and prayers they never left me."

Gwen V. of New York received a different, but no less important, type of return from her pet. "Clancy was with me through my turbulent teen years," she wrote. "He helped me through a great many broken hearts! When he died, I felt as if I'd lost my greatest confidante. Unlike human friends, he listened but didn't talk back with unwanted (no matter how correct) advice."

Think back upon some of the hard times you've shared with your pet. Can you remember times when it has stood by you when the rest of the world seemed to pass you by? Times when you came home feeling exhausted and beaten down by the events of the day, perhaps ready to cry from frustration, only to be cheered up by the loving welcome of your pet? Whether the traumas in your life have been major or, in retrospect, mundane, the presence of a pet has undoubtedly made them easier to bear. While you're at it, think of the good times, too—and how your pet made them even better. Small wonder that the loss of a pet is a major trauma in itself!

In many cases, a pet is its owner's only family or friend. Many pet owners, young and old, live alone. A pet owner may be cut off from other family members, perhaps by distance, perhaps by choice, perhaps because no other family is living. Many senior citizens would receive no love or companionship at all if it weren't for the pets in their lives—and the same can be said for many younger pet owners as well.

Human relationships are often difficult to form; some are even more difficult to maintain. Humans have arguments, moods, whims and often intolerable quirks; friends move away, spouses become bored with one another, families scatter across the country in pursuit of careers. Death, divorce and life's many transitions take their toll on human relationships. But when was the last time you and your dog had an argument about money, about your job, or about the type of restaurant you wanted to visit? When did your cat last criticize your hairstyle or your choice of television programs? A pet will cheerfully stick by you no matter where you go and regardless of the changes you make in your life. Such a creature has more than earned the title of "family member."

"I emphasize the unconditional love—like God's—that most of our companion animals give us and that most people are unable to give us," writes counselor Maurine J. Sauters. "Somehow I work in the fact that dog is God spelled backwards (unless the pet is other than a dog). Also, the love for a companion animal helps show us that love is a verb—love is doing for, feeling about, being with. We learn how to care, be kind and gentle, be responsible. We give without predetermining what we expect in return.

"The love of our animals for us can boost our self-esteem and our feelings of worth, because they never criticize or judge us. They love us as we are. Perhaps most of all, animals can teach humans how to receive love. For the elderly or the lonely, having a pet to care for and love and be loved by helps prove they are valuable persons, worthwhile, needed."

It may also help you in understanding your grief and its duration to consider the amount of time a pet has been a part of your life. If you're surprised that your sorrow has lasted so long—a week? a month? a year?—consider how long the pet was an integral part of your life.

"It's been just over a year and I can still see him running to me or sunning himself on the lawn," wrote Jacqueline R. of New York. Jacqueline's pet had been a part of her life for a long time indeed. "You see, I left home at 18, and I missed my family dog so much that I got Hurky. We were together for 14 years, and you couldn't find a better pal. I used to joke that I grew up with my dog instead of my family."

How many relationships have you had that lasted 14 years? These days, it seems few marriages hold together that long. I've known only one friend that long, and our contact is limited to cards at Christmas. So if you have been interacting with a pet on a daily basis, with the give-and-take of a truly loving relationship, for 14 years or even one year, don't be surprised by your inability to casually write off that relationship when the pet dies. As I mentioned earlier, the loss of a pet creates a genuine hole in your life, both physically and emotionally, and it will take considerable adjustment to ease the pain of that hole.

In the next chapter, we'll look at the ways in which that pain is likely to manifest itself, and at specific things you can do about it. There *is* a way out of the swamp!

Chapter 2

Emotional Reactions

I T WAS THE MOST TRAGIC, traumatic, and emotionally devastating experience my husband and I had ever been through. We didn't know what to do. We cried day and night." (Dorothy R., Alabama)

"I felt like someone had ripped out my insides." (Karen A., Illinois)

"I never knew anything could hurt so bad. I cried a whole ocean of tears. I went through self-hatred for putting my pet to sleep, to depression, to acceptance. For a long time I couldn't even watch a dog food commercial." (Cheryl T., Alabama)

"It hurt so much to let him go. You feel so helpless when a loving companion, a constant in your life, is taken away. Even though I did all I could to save him, I felt guilty. Then anger set in, mostly at the illness, then the pain as I realized the finality of it." (Susan K., New York)

Do these reactions to the loss of a pet touch a familiar chord in your heart? Grief, confusion, anger, guilt and depression are all typical responses to the death of a loved one; these emotions have been noted for years by researchers studying the effects of the loss of human loved ones and family members. Only recently, however, have researchers come to realize that a pet may also be considered a loved one and a family member, and that its death may evoke similar and often equally intense emotions.

This chapter will discuss some of the most typical reactions to the loss of a pet, as well as methods to cope with these feelings. Keep in mind, however, that there is no absolute pattern for grief. Your own reactions will depend on a variety of factors. These include your personality, your upbringing, the type of relationship you had with your pet, your personal situation at the time of the pet's death, and your cultural and religious beliefs. Your reactions may be different from those of another pet owner, or even from those of other members of your household. They may include some or all of the emotions listed above, in different combinations and intensities.

For example, if your dog died peacefully at the age of 16—a ripe old age for most dogs—the shock and grief you feel may be less than if it died of an unexpected illness at age 2. If your cat is hit by a car or your dog chokes on a bone, however, you will probably feel more guilt than you would if either pet had died of old age. You may feel the absence of a beloved companion more keenly and painfully if it was your only pet than if you shared your love with several animals. You may mourn the death of a particular pet more strongly than you mourned pets in the past, due to some special qualities of that pet or of that particular relationship.

The length of time grief lasts also varies from person to person, and may be affected by the level of attachment one feels to an individual pet. "My personal experience was an intense grieving process that left me emotionally devastated for several weeks," wrote Roanne H. of New Jersey. "I am still surprised by the ongoing feelings of love for the departed pet that I am experiencing. The length of time it takes to begin accepting the loss of your pet will vary."

Perhaps the most vital step in coping with the emotions you will feel upon the loss of your pet is *acknowledging* them. "Let yourself feel—write down your feelings, cry, be angry, call someone. Know that it is all right to be so upset over losing your pet and that it takes time to heal," wrote Susan K. of New York. "To deny and/or repress that sense of loss would be to devalue the love and affection that the pet brought into your life," said Pat H. of Pennsylvania.

You may run into people—even close friends—who don't understand your grief, and who may tell you that it is "silly" or "inappropriate" to grieve over the loss of an animal. After all, it was "just a dog." It is easy to condemn such people out of hand for what seems to you an inexcusable lack of understanding. But before you write off these friends or acquaintances, remind yourself that few people have much experience in dealing with grief, either their own or that of others. Grief makes people uncomfortable; most people genuinely want to help, but simply don't know how—and they are painfully aware that they lack the right words to console you or make you feel better. The words they do find may seem clumsy or insensitive to you.

It's also a good idea to keep in mind that many, many people have simply never had a close relationship with an animal of any kind. Perhaps their parents never allowed them to have pets as children, so they grew up without knowing how much animals can mean in our lives. Different people live different lives; be aware of the differences between your experiences and those of people who seem insensitive to your loss. If you can, seek out those people who have had similar relationships with pets—but remember, even other pet lovers may not be experts at dealing with the emotional needs of other humans!

"The problem is that our culture is extremely intolerant of grief," writes California animal behaviorist C. Miriam Yarden. "From childhood we are taught that crying is a show of weakness—and in the case of boys and men this attitude is even more rigid. We often do not allow our children to mourn or feel a loss, let alone show it. Most often it is such owners who espouse the attitude of hard determination to never get another pet because 'I can't go through this again.' Of course they can't go through this 'again,' considering that they haven't gone through 'this' in the first place! It is also they who suffer the most."

You may not wish to admit the strength of your reactions even to yourself. If, for example, you think it is silly or weak to feel such overwhelming grief, you may try to convince yourself that you aren't feeling it, that everything is fine. Kathi W. of Florida is one of many pet owners who has realized the danger of this course of action. "I have come to learn that it is natural to feel grief over the loss of anything we attach ourselves to emotionally," she wrote. "No matter how large or small our loss may be, we must openly discuss our feelings or our grief will not be resolved. By attempting to ignore our pain, we may become withdrawn and face serious medical and psychological problems at a later date."

You can't begin to cope with your emotions until you let them out. If you feel guilt, you can't address the cause of the guilt or find a solution to it if you are busily saying "What, me, guilt? No—everything's great!" For decades psychologists and psychiatrists have been pointing out the dangers of repressing, ignoring or denying emotions. Repressed emotions don't go away simply because you don't want to admit they are there—instead, when denied an outlet, emotions churn around inside you until they find their own outlet—often when you least expect it and are least prepared to handle it. If you deny your anger over the death of your dog, it doesn't go away: Instead, you may flare up and shout at your child or your husband for no reason, causing more hurt and misunderstanding. Since that outlet still doesn't bring what's really bothering you into the open, the cause of the anger or other emotion isn't resolved, so it continues to churn inside you. I have heard from pet owners whose unresolved emotions have kept them bitter and hurting for years.

Acknowledging your emotions may hurt—these emotions are painful, after all—but it provides you with the opportunity to control their outlet. You may decide, for example, that you need to take a day off from work and simply cry your heart out, scream your anger to the skies, or pound out your guilt on the floor. Far from being childish, this action lets you get your feelings into the open. There you can look at them and begin to understand them, which is a healthy start on releasing them once and for all. Only by looking at your reactions honestly can you begin the process of working through them and coming out whole and happy on the other side.

"Grief consists of several steps, which ought to be taken one at a time," Yarden says. "It is also an experience that will recur over and over after a loss, and through that repetition comes the slow easing of pain. Each time, one experiences a little more consolation, a little more healing. Some of the stages one goes through are shock, denial, anger, loneliness, self-pity, guilt, and regret—to name a few. Everyone who has lost a loved relative or close friend experiences loneliness and the feeling that no one can fill the emptiness that person left behind. One may suffer from guilt, thinking that one 'should have' or 'could have' or 'might have' done certain things while the lost friend was still alive. The feeling of anger is at ourselves for not having noticed that something was amiss, for not having sought medical help sooner—or it is sometimes redirected at the deceased for dying and leaving us."

Of the complex jumble of emotions that may follow the death of a pet, four stand out as being particularly difficult to acknowledge or understand, and therefore to work through: anger, guilt, denial and depression. A pet owner who "sticks" at one of these reactions faces a major obstacle in the grief swamp. If you find yourself dwelling on one of these emotions, or spending an inordinate amount of time "denying" the emotion, it is important to work on a more realistic understanding of the situation. Otherwise, your feelings may distort your entire perspective on the loss of your pet and your role in its death, and seriously hinder your recovery.

Anger

When a person is hurt, a natural response is to look around for the person or thing that is causing that hurt. Pain is something one often sees as being inflicted from outside, rather than something that just happens. Historically, when no obvious cause for trouble is found, people have made scapegoats out of strangers, supernatural forces, or even God. Finding something or someone to blame for one's pain enables one to "strike back," if only by declaring, "It's your fault, you did it."

Focusing anger on a target of blame is a distraction. On her national radio talk show, psychologist Toni Grant often noted that a person can focus on only one strong emotion at a time; thus, if you have focused all your energy into anger, you have little time to feel your pain. Striking back can be gratifying; you may get a surge of satisfaction from telling off your "persecutor." But acknowledging your pain is an essential part of the grieving process, so while the distraction of anger may temporarily seem to ease your feelings, in the long run it only serves to prolong an already difficult situation.

Whom can you blame for the death of a pet? Pet owners have come up with a surprising number of possibilities. They may blame pet deaths on veterinarians, animal shelters, the person who caused a fatal accident or injury, the illness that was responsible for the death, and even the pet itself.

Veterinarians frequently come under fire for the loss of a pet, because a vet is often the last person to be responsible for a sick or injured pet. Instead of asking the logical question, "Why couldn't you save my pet?" a grieving pet owner may ask, "Why *didn't* you save my pet?" as though the veterinarian had a choice. Since so many treatments seem virtual miracles, why couldn't the vet have pulled off the final miracle needed to keep a beloved pet alive? To some, this failure may seem deliberate, neglectful or uncaring.

Susan G. of Nebraska blamed her veterinarian bitterly for the death of her St. Bernard, Junior. "Was surgery the only alternative?" she wrote. "At the time it seemed that we could trust this vet. Now I feel he couldn't have cared less about my baby! We thought he would save Junior's life. Instead I felt like he murdered him and put him through torture by that surgery... If he felt his surgery might kill my dog, why did he decide on it in the end? Do they do this just so they can practice on helpless animals?"

To read Susan's letter is to read the story of a dog with virtually no chance of survival—but to Susan, the dog's killer is the tangible, accessible veterinarian who had the final responsibility for her pet, not the mysterious disease that brought the dog to the hospital in the first place. Two years after her original letter, Susan wrote to me again, and her anger and pain still simmered beneath the surface: "I feel I will always be bitter about what happened and I could never trust any professional (medical or other) again!"

An assumption of negligence, ignorance, cruelty or lack of care on the part of a veterinarian makes the death of a loved one easier to understand than if one had to write it off to fate or an incomprehensible act of God. It makes the question of "why did this have to happen to me?" or "why did my pet have to die?" easier to answer, enabling one to say, "Well, it wouldn't have happened if only..."

When Laura P. of California lost her pit bull puppy to parvovirus only a few days after she adopted it from an animal shelter, she felt considerable anger toward the shelter. "They were so concerned about whether I had a secure yard that they didn't even notice the pup was losing weight and getting dehydrated," she wrote. Yvonne M. of New Jersey had a similar experience, and demanded, "Why does the state allow such places to exist?" She was infuriated by the shelter's promise to replace a pet if anything went wrong. "How can you develop a love for an animal and then replace it awhile later?" she asks.

If someone causes the death of your pet through a malicious act or through carelessness, it's certainly natural to feel anger toward that person. When Vivian R.'s dog was shot near its New Hampshire home, "all my husband and I could think of was to go home and find whoever did this terrible thing," she wrote. Vivian's situation demonstrates the need to maintain a level of common sense along with one's anger. She and her husband did locate the shooter, a neighbor, who was eventually required to pay damages. She stopped short, however, of having the man arrested because of her concern for the suffering this would cause the man's wife and two young children, who had nothing to do with the incident.

In this case, Vivian's anger was channeled into a constructive action that eventually cleared the way for her grief and for sympathy toward others. But Vivian was fortunate: She and her husband were able to track down the person responsible and had the legal resources to achieve a certain amount of justice, though no amount of money can ever replace a lost pet. All too often, the person who caused the death of a pet cannot be found, or no legal means of retaliation may be open to you. You may cause yourself far more suffering if you try to retaliate by taking the law into your own hands. If you are spending an inordinate amount of time concentrating on rage and hatred toward the faceless, untraceable driver of the speeding car that struck down your pet, you may be seriously impeding your recovery from your loss.

Some people feel anger toward the illness that kills a pet. It isn't fair; why did it have to happen to *this* pet? One person wrote that she felt fate had played a cruel trick on her: Her dog died of coronavirus just weeks before she read a magazine article about the disease and the new vaccine that had been developed for it.

It is even possible to feel anger toward the dead pet itself. "The only time she ever hurt me was when she left me," wrote one pet owner. You may feel angry at it for dying and leaving you, thus causing you pain, or for doing something that caused its own death. For example, if your pet escaped from the yard and ran into the road at the wrong time, or ate a poisonous plant, or provoked a fight with another animal, you may blame the pet for the "stupidity" that took it from you.

One pet owner felt a certain amount of anger toward her dog for appearing perfectly healthy on the morning of its death. This pet owner felt that if only the dog had shown, somehow, that something was wrong, the owner would not have left it home alone but would have taken it to the vet, who might have been able to save it. If no other target is available, the pet may become the focus of blame for the anger and hurt you're feeling at this time.

You may also feel anger toward yourself, perhaps seeing yourself as the cause of the pet's death. Anger turned inward, into self-blame, becomes guilt.

Guilt

By becoming the caretaker of an animal, one may come to feel responsible for everything that happens to that animal, including events beyond one's control. Thus, if something goes wrong, whether the owner has anything to do with or not, he is likely to feel responsible—and therefore guilty.

I heard from several owners who blamed themselves for some "terrible mistake," real or imagined, that caused a pet's death. Kathy D. of Oklahoma wrote, "Cause of death: It was my fault. She died of distemper and had never been vaccinated." Shirley O. of California said, "I had a terrible time adjusting to the loss of my dog; the underlying factor was my guilt. I had ignorantly fed my dog soft pork chop bones, not knowing they'd cause intestinal hemorrhage."

If you must make the decision to euthanize a sick or injured pet, this can cause a tremendous amount of guilt. This type of guilt, and euthanasia in general, are covered in more detail in Chapter Six. Susan G., who felt such anger toward her veterinarian over the death of her dog, offers a heart-wrenching example of the guilt euthanasia can evoke: "How could I have been so ignorant with something I loved?" she wrote. "I felt it was wrong to leave him there from the first day; now I hold it against them and myself... I'm the one who took him there. Every day is a living hell when I think about what I put Junior through... I feel like he trusted me and I let him down."

Sue K. also felt considerable guilt when she had her cat Titsie euthanized, but as she discovered, that guilt extended far beyond the act of ending her cat's life. "I doubted my decision," she wrote. "Maybe I could have managed him at home. Maybe I should have tried. Maybe I shouldn't have taken him to the vet college. I'm a nurse; I should have noticed his failing condition. Why didn't I pay more attention? I shouldn't have gotten the new kitten; he tired Titsie so. And the dog! Titsie had hated Katie so much toward the end, and Katie had taken up so much of my attention because dogs demand more by their very nature. Maybe God was punishing me for something by taking Titsie away; Lord knows I'm no saint. That was probably it. I should be kinder. I should try harder to be better. I should watch what I say. I should have lived a better life. It was all my fault. I had killed my cat by not being what I should be."

Despite such intense feelings of guilt and self-hate, Sue was able to work her way back to solid ground; her letter was a testimonial to the powers of recovery that lie within us. "It's been only three months since Titsie died," she concluded, "and it was difficult at times to see the typewriter through my tears. But these were honest tears—tears of missing Titsie and of remembering his death and how alone I felt—not the distorted tears of self-blame, guilt, and hopelessness."

Even if a pet owner can't pinpoint something about the pet's death to feel guilty about, he may find something else to focus on—just as Sue focused on her supposed inadequacies. He may decide that he didn't take good enough care of the pet while it was alive, or pay enough attention to it. This is part of the "if only" syndrome: "If only I had known you wouldn't be here tomorrow, I would have been nicer to you yesterday."

Laura P. of California, who lost two dogs she had owned since age 7, expressed this type of guilt in her letter: "I felt sad and heartbroken, but mostly I felt guilty for any and all bad things I had done to Tiny and Pebbles over their lifetimes. When I was younger I just didn't respect my pets and was mean. I remembered the times I ignored them or forgot to give them water. I cried remembering the times I would just say 'hi' through the back screen instead of petting their little heads or scratching their tummies. I cried thinking of the times they needed brushing or a walk but had the gate closed in their faces. I cried thinking of how little they asked in return for their loyalty and love. I will never again shun any dog for getting old; in fact, I want to devote my life to dogs, training them and telling others how to care for them."

Just as anger can make you unable to recover from grief because it diverts your attention from your deeper, more painful reactions, guilt can be an equally dangerous distraction. Guilt causes you to focus on your supposed inadequacies and failings rather than on the reality of your loss. Though anger can distract from your pain, guilt adds to it by convincing you that, since you are at fault, you "deserve" to suffer. Guilt distorts your self-image, destroying your self-confidence and undermining your strength. Instead of focusing on the positive aspects of your relationship with your pet and on the happy memories, you focus upon the negative memories (real or imagined), the pet's illness or death and your "bad guy" role in it.

Even if you *did* make some tragic mistake or decision that caused the death of your pet, clinging to guilt not only prevents you from recovering from your grief, it prevents you from moving on to a better and wiser relationship with future pets. Guilt does not help your departed pet, it does not help you, and it does not help any pets you may own in the future. Instead of helping you learn and grow from the experience of your mistakes, guilt drags you deeper into pain and, if carried to extremes, can block your route out of the grief-swamp.

Denial

Like anger, denial can be a way of focusing your mind away

from pain. Denial is not so much a distraction, however, as a mechanism of ignoring reality, of hoping that if you don't feel the pain, it will go away. Unfortunately, this rarely works; instead, pain is likely to wait until you let your defense mechanism slip, and then lash out at you when you are least prepared to cope with it.

Denial has been described in detail by researchers who study the terminally ill. Dr. Elizabeth Kubler-Ross, in her landmark book *On Death and Dying*, noted that dying patients would often insist that they were not ill or that they were getting better. The reality of impending death is, understandably, often too painful to accept on a conscious level. Denial is a way of avoiding the mental anguish that comes with the realization that death is inevitable.

Pet owners often practice a similar type of denial. C. Miriam Yarden wrote of a woman whose dog was diagnosed as being terminally ill. Whenever Yarden asked the woman about the dog, the woman insisted that the dog was fine, that it was getting better, that nothing was wrong with it. In a few months the dog died, and the woman was devastated. In a case such as this, denial robs a pet owner of vital time in which he could be preparing himself emotionally for the inevitable loss and trauma that is to come.

Carried to extremes, denial can even be physically harmful to a pet. Just as a human patient may fearfully deny the seriousness of his symptoms and postpone visiting a doctor until it is too late to halt the course of an illness, so might a pet owner deny the seriousness of a pet's symptoms until it is too late for a veterinarian to help. Even when one does take the pet to the vet, ignoring the seriousness of the illness can lead to significant problems in coping later, as Celia P. of New York discovered.

"You must be realistic," wrote Celia. "Cam had blood in his urine periodically for a long time. We convinced ourselves that it was the same old urinary problem that he'd had before. Not smart. Pretending that an aging animal is going on forever just makes it harder to accept the final outcome. We just 'tuned out' any suggestion from the vet that this could be something more serious (it was cancer) and stuck to the old 'he's got a bladder problem—probably passed a stone again' assumption.

Please don't do this; it just makes the shock a hundred times worse."

Denial can also take place on a subconscious level. You may know, intellectually, that your pet is dead, but at a gut level be unable to accept that fact. You may still believe that somehow you will see your pet again; you might fear, for example, that your pet was not actually euthanized and is still alive somewhere. (That's why many pet owners recommend that you stay with your pet during euthanasia, a point that will be discussed in Chapter Six.) I experienced this feeling upon the death of my cat; even though I had held his body in my arms and said good-bye to him, I still found myself watching the streets for him at night as I drove home from work. A part of me seemed to have stuck at the memory that he had not come home that night, while refusing to accept the memory of the discovery of his body.

Denial can surface when you contemplate obtaining a new pet. You may find that this decision makes you feel guilty or disloyal, as though you were somehow betraying the deceased pet's memory. This reaction may mean that in a very real sense, you have not let go of the old pet, for it is still alive enough in your mind to be "replaced" by a "usurper." Bringing a new pet into your home can be the ultimate admission that your old pet is gone; we'll discuss ways to handle this emotional trauma in Chapter Five.

Depression

Though depression can result from a variety of things, including purely physical causes, we often associate this condition with an event or ongoing situation that has caused significant emotional pain or high levels of stress. This type of depression can range from a sense of "feeling low" to what can amount to a state of emotional near-paralysis. It can last for a few hours or a day—or drag on for weeks and months.

The death of a pet is certainly the type of event that one would expect to trigger depression. It is traumatic, painful and stressful; it creates a situation that plunges a person into a whirlpool of emotions, and is an event that one may very well wish to withdraw from rather than confront. But, though depression is a logical result of pet loss, it is also a state of mind that can impede a pet owner's recovery from that loss.

Shirley O., who felt such guilt over feeding her dog the bones that caused its death, also suffered from the classic symptoms of depression. "The sudden death of my dog left me so devastated that I'd walk around the house wringing my hands and crying," she wrote. "I lost my appetite and powers of concentration, and wondered if I was losing my mind." A California pet owner experienced another typical manifestation of depression: She found herself virtually unable to carry on with her day-to-day routines. "Frankly, I didn't get much done and had lost interest in living," she wrote. Even getting out of bed, eating and performing simple tasks was an effort. Severe depression can make living seem intolerable, and rob one of the willpower and strength to put forth even the most minimal of efforts.

Shirley's situation was a little unusual: Three months before the death of her dog, her husband had died of a lengthy illness. She felt considerably more anguish over the death of the dog than of her husband, and wondered if perhaps the dog's death had triggered pent-up feelings that she had not released the first time through. She discounted that possibility, however. "My husband had wanted to die for years," she wrote, "and made himself and those around him so miserable that it was a relief when he didn't suffer anymore."

Despite Shirley's disclaimer, it seems likely that the death of her dog was the proverbial hole in the dike that let a whole flood of painful emotions, perhaps bottled up for years, burst through. It also seems likely that, due to the difficulties in her marital relationship, Shirley developed an unusually strong bond with her dog, who probably provided the love and support that was not forthcoming elsewhere.

This type of situation is not as uncommon as it might sound. If your life is in turmoil—if, for instance, problems are occurring in relationships or careers or family situations—your relationship with your pet may be the only stable thing in your life. No matter how bad things get everywhere else, a pet will continue to offer unconditional love and acceptance.

Even when the trying times or stressful changes are past, you may still feel an intense attachment to that pet. "I couldn't have survived without him," you might say. "He was my good luck charm." You might even fear that your life will fall apart completely without that "anchor," even if the crises that the pet anchored you through have long since resolved themselves. If they haven't been resolved, the loss of the pet can be even more traumatic, because you may then feel completely cut off from any source of love and support.

Thus the loss of a pet should be viewed not just as an independent event, but in the context of your life at the time of the loss. If you find yourself reacting far more severely to the loss than you anticipated—perhaps more severely than you have reacted to deaths of earlier pets—you might wish to examine other possible sources of stress in your life. Was your pet helping you cope with painful emotions arising from some other problem? Has the death of the pet left you not only with your grief over its loss, but with an unpleasant situation or backlog of stress that you must now face alone, without the pet's "moral support"? If you can, try to separate the bereavement trauma from other crises in your life and allot some time to it alone, so that you can view it from a perspective that is not magnified and distorted by external events.

The depression that results from this type of situation, or even from the loss of a pet without outside complications, makes a constructive approach to handling your grief difficult. One of the symptoms of depression is a lack of energy, an inability to focus even on simple things, let alone on the overwhelming problem of your grief. While it is not a good idea to distract yourself from your grief to the point of ignoring or denying its existence, one tried-and-true coping strategy is to focus on outside activities: your work, friends, a change of scene. This type of healthy distraction keeps you in touch with reality, which helps keep your grief and loss in perspective. But depression robs you of the energy or inclination to pursue even trivial activities, creating a spiral effect: If you cannot distract yourself from grief, you tend to dwell upon it, which makes the depression worse, which makes it even more difficult to break out of the cycle, and so forth.

Powerful emotions are an integral part of grief. You won't be able to avoid them, and in some cases, in the right proportions, these emotions can be helpful to you in negotiating the grief-swamp. Constructive anger, for example, can help you resolve the situation that caused your pet's death, giving you a feeling of accomplishment. However, anger that you hold onto because you can't focus it constructively can make you feel helpless, and hinder your progress. Blind anger will simply send you charging off wildly through the swamp or keep you running in circles.

Guilt has few benefits; however, Kathi D.'s guilt over her failure to immunize her dog caused her to be much more careful with subsequent pets. If you *are* somehow responsible for the death of your pet, your sense of guilt is useful only so far as it prompts you to correct the error—fix the fence, keep your next cat indoors, never feed bones to another dog. But if guilt causes you to focus on your own supposed worthlessness and inadequacies, you trap yourself in the swamp by convincing yourself that you're such a lowlife scum that you belong there.

Denial can help you on a brief, temporary basis by letting you shift your attention away from emotions that are, for the moment, too painful to bear. It's perfectly acceptable, for instance, to say, "I won't think about what just happened right now, because I have to drive home on the freeway, and I'll fall apart and be unable to function if I don't put it out of my mind. I'll fall apart when I get home, instead." But if you try to deny the situation for a longer period of time or altogether, beware: The swamp hasn't gone away just because you have closed your eyes and told yourself that it doesn't exist. You are still in the middle of it, and by walking on blindly you may step in quicksand when you least expect it.

Depression could surely be described as quicksand. It is a natural reaction, and justified by the nature of your loss. But if you feel the symptoms of depression taking hold of you to the extent that they interfere with your day-to-day life, you need to make every possible effort to break out of it before it becomes a trap. This isn't easy to accomplish alone; if you can, enlist the help of friends and relatives to keep you "moving" and distracted. Even if your friends don't understand the cause of your grief, let them know that you need their help and support regardless. It's impossible to even begin to make your way out of the swamp if you're sinking slowly into a patch of quicksand.

At this point you may be thinking, "It's all very well for her to say, 'Do this' and 'Don't think that,' but how can I help what I'm feeling? If I have these feelings, what can I do about them?" The next chapter will give you some answers to that question by presenting some coping strategies that have been used successfully by pet owners like yourself.

"Like all counselors, I am often asked, 'When will I get over this? Will I ever get over this?'" writes Muriel Franzblau of the Bide-A-Wee Home Association. "Though my answer is frequently surprising to clients, I've seen it work well time and time again: 'You won't get over it. I don't believe we ever "get over" the loss of someone we've loved so much. But you'll do something much better. Gradually, and in your own time, you'll make peace with yourself and then you'll make peace with your loss. And you'll go on from there.'"

Coping with sorrow is easier said than done—but it has been done, and you can do it too.

Chapter 3

Coping
Strategies

ONE OF THE MOST DIFFICULT ASPECTS of bereavement is the sense of hopelessness it causes. When you are grieving over the loss of a pet, it is very easy to believe that this emotional state will continue forever. After all, your loss is forever; your pet will never come back to you. You may find it hard to imagine ever feeling less miserable than you feel now. The cliches those around you may utter in their attempts to console you, such as "stop thinking about it," "time heals all wounds" and "you'll get over it eventually," sound meaningless at a time like this.

Though you may not be able to accept these statements at a gut level, however, it's wise to keep in mind that they do contain an element of truth. Time *is* the only real cure for grief: No matter what coping strategy you use, there is no instant remedy for your pain. While you can't stop thinking about your loss, dwelling on it excessively or getting caught up in one of the reactions described in the preceding chapter will hinder, rather than help, your progress. And though it may not seem possible now, if you take active steps to help yourself through the bereavement process, you *will* get over your pain in time. The length of time may vary; as Carol F. of

Kentucky points out, "Grief progresses at different rates for different people. You cannot rush it, but you must allow yourself to accept the reality of it."

As I mentioned in Chapter One, recovery is a two-pronged process. The first prong is understanding your emotional reactions to your loss, and Chapter Two was designed to help you do just that. In this chapter, we'll look at the importance of accepting your emotions, and at ways you can focus them in a more positive direction.

The second prong is readjusting your life so that the hole created by the absence of your pet is less noticeable and, therefore, less painful. It's important to understand, however, that these two phases are not separate, but should be worked on at the same time. Your emotions are tied in with the absence of your pet, so whatever progress you make in one of these areas will help you in the other.

There is no one "right way" to cope with grief. You may find that all of the coping strategies listed below help you, or that some help you more than others, or that one particular strategy makes "all the difference." The secret lies not so much in discovering the perfect coping strategy as in discovering that you actually have choices in the first place—that you are not trapped in the grief swamp with no way out.

Acknowledging Your Feelings

1. Let yourself grieve. I mentioned the importance of acknowledging and expressing your emotions in Chapter Two. Not surprisingly, this was the recommendation pet owners repeated over and over as the single most important part of coping with pet loss. Many pet owners had experienced lack of understanding on the part of relatives and friends, and know that it can be embarrassing to show your feelings in front of people who don't care about pets the way you do. Do it anyway, these pet owners urged; don't worry about what people think, and don't let people try to tell you what to feel.

"Don't be afraid to cry and let out your feelings," wrote Beth N. of New Hampshire. "I think this is extremely important, especially for older owners. It seems that as you get older, no one wants to see you cry over a pet. Express your feelings whether people like it or not. Talk to someone who might know how you feel. Let it all out!"

Cathy W. of Wisconsin agreed. "Most importantly," she wrote, "do not let people intimidate you into feeling embarrassed or ashamed about your grief and tears. My two teenage sons did not understand my feelings and thought I was being rather 'immature' and 'childish.' Stand your ground, let them know how you feel and insist that they keep their callous comments to themselves."

"The feelings you have toward your pet are genuine and deep," reminds Carol F. "You need not be embarrassed about them or feel childish or ashamed. As with any grief, it is important to acknowledge the loss and its meaning to you personally. It is important to allow yourself to cry, to drag out pictures, to talk with a sympathetic person about how special this pet was to you. In this way you can work through the initial stages of grief. Let yourself feel the loss and the absence of the loved one."

Remember that your pet is a loved one, no matter what type of creature it may be. "My husband understood that I had lost not a horse, but a deeply loved individual, friend and companion," wrote D.E. of Georgia. "Others, even though they knew me well, could not understand the sorrow and love I had for my Lady. I cried and mourned for over three months for Lady. But gradually the acute pain fades and then you remember the good times together."

2. Remember the good times. D.E. wasn't the only pet owner to suggest this coping strategy: As dozens of pet owners pointed out, focusing on the good memories and the happy times you shared with your pet is one of the best ways to shift your thoughts away from your pain. "Always remember your friend in a good way," wrote Beth N. "Not while it was sick, but while it was well and doing things with you. I think you should remember that you were its best friend and that it loved you very much."

"God does not want us to concentrate on the death of a pet, but to concentrate, with His help, on the pet while it was alive, and on all the fun and enjoyment we had with it," wrote Alvin W. of Indiana. "This pet can be alive in our hearts, even though it is gone."

"I found that reminiscing about the good times helped me

feel good and made going through the inevitable loss worthwhile," agreed Mary Z. of California.

Minta S. of Texas shared some of the memories she and her husband reminisce about. "As we plan our upcoming vacations, we remember how our German Shepherd, Ermingarde, loved to travel," she wrote. "During her 14 years she traveled with us from the West Coast to the East Coast, as far north as mid-Canada and as far south as Guatemala. We remember how content Que-Ling, our beloved cat, was on our trips, too. We smile and say things like, 'If Ermie and Que were here, they'd sure be going crazy, seeing us pack the trailer.' And we wonder what kind of traveler our new dog will be. This is the way to live with the loss of a beloved family member: remembering, still loving, but not unduly grieving, and sharing what we have to give with those animals still living and needing it."

While you think about the good times you shared with your pets—the walks, the romps, the quiet evenings of shared affection—it can also be helpful to think about the good you did for your pet during its lifetime, especially if you are feeling guilt for its death. Did you adopt your pet from an animal shelter? Think about the many happy years of life you gave an animal that might otherwise have become another "unwanted pet" statistic. Did you take good care of your pet? Though Cheryl F. of Florida was grieved by the loss of her pets, she realized: "I must have done something right or they wouldn't all have lived so long." Maintaining a positive attitude about yourself and your role in your pet's life is one of the healthiest things you can do for yourself.

3. Seek outside help. If you are having trouble coping with your feelings on your own, you may want to get some help. Help can come from a variety of sources: friends, secular and religious counselors, doctors, veterinarians, and even books like this one. Before you reject this idea as a sign of weakness or inability to handle your own problems, keep in mind that it has always been acceptable to turn to others for help and consolation when a human loved one dies. Unfortunately, the support systems that help a grieving survivor cope with a human loss are not well-established for the loss of a non-human loved one. But if you feel as much pain over the death of a pet as over any other type of family loss, you have just as much right to look for help and support from others.

"I think a person should have a support group to rely on until the worst is over: immediate family, close friends, or someone they can trust who may work at the animal hospital where the pet was a patient," wrote Katie K. of Florida. "Stick with friends who can empathize with you and cry with you," agreed Mary P. of Louisiana. "Since I don't or won't have friends who don't love animals, this has helped. I avoid those people who don't love animals; they certainly aren't what you need when you have just lost a 'family member.'"

"If possible, make an effort to be around other 'dog people' who can really understand your feelings," suggested Barbara T. of New Jersey. "Being able to take my Belgian Sheepdog to her regular obedience class and talk about the 12-year-old Sheltie mix that had been put down made it easier for me to accept the decision I had made."

Your veterinarian may be a sympathetic ear in your time of need, especially if he or she has developed a relationship with your pet over the years. Many veterinarians care deeply about their furry patients, and are truly grieved when a long-time client and friend dies. Animal clinic staff members who have seen a pet through a long illness may experience a sense of loss themselves when the animal finally succumbs. These professionals, who have had to deal with many such tragedies, are often glad to provide a sympathetic ear or some words of counsel when you need it most.

Many pet owners wrote that they had benefited tremendously from the help of a bereavement counselor or group therapy session for bereaved pet owners. "When you are with other people who have recently lost animals and who are grieving, it is possible to openly express the grief," wrote Anne R. of New York. "Listening and providing support to others is also nourishing to the empty heart at this time. With the help of the group I was able to get through that horrible time and have another pet. I really believe I would still be in pain if it weren't for this. Pet loss cannot be handled alone. The cruelty I encountered from others was certainly balanced by the support I received from the group."

Shirley visited the hospice department of the hospital

where her husband had died; the counselors there were trained to handle a survivor's grief, whether the loss was human or animal. If you seek a counselor, look for someone who has an understanding of the needs of a pet owner. Check the yellow pages for a counselor in your area, and ask veterinarians, local animal shelters, animal behaviorists and other pet-care professionals for referrals. If no counselors specializing in pet loss are available in your area, check with local hospitals to find out if they have a grief counselor who could help you. Check with churches and social agencies. Chances are, even if you don't find the professional help you're looking for, in all this checking you'll find at least one sympathetic person who can provide you with some of the support you need!

4. Turn to your faith. Often, a belief in God, an afterlife, or in a divine purpose in all things has helped pet owners develop their own answers to questions like "Why did my pet have to die?" and "Will we ever be reunited?" Faith can help a pet owner sort through some of the pain and confusion pet loss causes.

"I just have to tell you what the only thing to help me was: Yes, God!" wrote Alvin W. "There are some things in life we cannot handle alone. God is loving and understanding of our feelings. He created both us and our pets. He understands that since we are emotional creatures, we will fall in love with our pets. If we will lean on and trust in Him, God will give us the strength we need."

"I truly believe my dog is in heaven, happy and content," said Sharon S. of Texas. "I know when I die, I'll join her. I don't see it any other way."

"I firmly believe that God would not have given us these wonderful, loving creatures only to deny them to us in heaven," agreed Eva D. of Arizona. "They are His creations too, and He loves them all. Believe that God has provided for our beloved pets in heaven, just as He has provided for us."

Kathy D. of Oklahoma had a beautiful answer to the questions many pet owners raise about pet loss. "The first thing I did was pray for understanding. The Bible doesn't really say whether animals go to heaven, and I felt I had to know. The answer the Lord gave me: He made my pets. He created in me the special love I feel for them. He loves them and takes care of them through me, and even beyond my own ability to take care of them—there is always, sometimes miraculously, money for the veterinarian or whatever they need.

"What are my pets, really? I won't spend eternity in a corruptible body; surely God would condemn no animal to that either. What if that spirit I love in my pet is actually that of an angel? Would I want an angel to be required to spend eternity in the body of a dog or cat, just to please me? And it would be many angels, as I've had many pets.

"I felt the Lord was telling me that I can fully trust Him to take care of my pets after their bodies die. If I need one or more pets in heaven, He will provide them, even as He has here on earth. Possibly one or more glorious animals, beyond my wildest dreams, encompassing the spirits of all the pets I have loved on earth. In heaven I'll never have a pet die again."

Many pet owners have asked me if I believed that pets go to heaven. Children often ask this question as well, and it's important to realize how comforting it can be to a grieving child to be able to hope that he will be reunited with his beloved pet one day. But that comfort isn't limited to children; a great many adult pet owners seek that comfort as well!

Nor are pet owners alone in seeking answers to this question. In a survey of veterinarians conducted in 1987, by Dr. Bruce Fogle, DVM, found that 19 percent of veterinarians surveyed believed that animals have souls, and 18 percent believed that there is an afterlife for pets.

Personally, I *do* believe that pets may go to heaven. However, when I'm asked that question by someone who wants more than my personal opinion but the support of Biblical references as well, the matter becomes a bit more complicated. As Kathy D. pointed out, the Bible doesn't really answer that question—and it is dangerous to base dogmatic answers upon an issue where scripture is silent. While many Christian thinkers have maintained over the centuries that animals don't have souls and therefore don't go to heaven, the simple truth is that *we don't know*—and we won't know until we get there!

An honest "I don't know" is a great deal more comforting than a dogmatic "absolutely not"—especially if the person asking the question is a child. As we grow older, we may come to believe, as Kathy says, that we may *not* need the same sort of emotional support from pets in heaven that we sometimes need here on earth, but this degree of faith is hard to achieve even for an adult, let alone a grieving child. My advice to anyone is to avoid the temptation to turn the death of a pet into a Valuable Learning Experience. Remember, the simple act of giving comfort (to children *or* adults) can provide a far more valuable and memorable lesson than dogma and doctrine!

5. Be prepared. Often it isn't possible to prepare in advance for the death of a pet, but the more you can do to prepare your emotions for this shock, the better off you will be. As Celia noted in Chapter Two, if you observe that your pet is old and sick, don't try to ignore its condition in an effort to avoid the pain of contemplating the eventual loss of your pet. That loss is inevitable, and closing your eyes to it will not prevent it from happening.

Beverly W. of Connecticut wrote, "A person who has developed a special relationship with a pet through the years should begin thinking about dealing with its inevitable loss when the pet is around 5 years of age. Considering the natural lifespan of a dog, death before that is unusual and death after that is more difficult, because though the years 'sweeten' the relationship, they also add to the memories that initially cause the pain." Beverly also urges that one "think about the next pet before the death of the present one. This enables one to make a wiser decision. When your mind is clouded with grief, you cannot think clearly, and that's why it should be dealt with as much as possible beforehand."

Cathy W. suggests that once one knows a pet's death is imminent, the intervening time can be used as a preparation for the loss. "Actually, we grieved throughout Trina's last 8-1/2 months, while we watched an active, fun-loving, obedience-loving dog waste away, becoming more and more ill each week. The heartache and pain during those months were great and a great number of tears were shed. I believe this long period of 'grieving' actually made the final decision easier."

When Cathy and her family finally decided that the time for euthanasia had come, "We made the appointment for two days later. This period of time gave me an opportunity to come to grips with the reality of the situation and accept it. If you have the luxury of time, make the appointment a few days in advance, because a couple of days can give you the time to accept the inevitable. It may also make you really look at your pet in a different way, and you may see suffering and pain you weren't aware of before."

It is also a good idea to make arrangements for the final disposal of your pet's body in advance. "Be prepared," urges Janet B. of Kansas. "Decide what you want to do with your pet before it becomes ill or injured. Whatever a pet owner wants for his pet, it is easier to cope with the situation if the decision has already been made. Whatever a person does to prepare himself for the death of a pet doesn't really ease the pain, but it does reduce the stress a person is under in such a situation, making it easier to cope." Chapter Seven offers suggestions on ways to prepare in advance for the final disposition of your beloved pet.

Finally, prepare by giving your pet all the love you can while it is alive. "I have a female Sheltie who follows me from room to room, constantly at my feet when I'm dressing, cleaning or doing dishes," wrote Lee Ann of Georgia. "This can be very annoying at times, but then I think, someday she won't be here to do this. I believe this is life's way of saying 'Don't take me for granted. Nothing is permanent in this world; live each day to the fullest. Enjoy and take care of what you have today, because tomorrow it may not be here.'"

Adjusting to Your Loss

1. Rearrange your surroundings. When a beloved pet is gone for good, nothing can bring back its memory as sharply as the sight of its bed, one of its toys, or even just a spot that it loved to sleep or play in. "When you first lose your pet, everything around your home reminds you of it," wrote Beth of New Hampshire. "It is hard to walk past places where it used to sleep and play without seeing it there. Take time to go away overnight or for a few days if possible. This gives you time to grieve in your own way, away from familiar things. When you come home, rearrange the rooms a little. Change things so that you are not always looking for your pet in the places where it always stayed. This helped me, because every time I went by his bed, I would start to think about his last night with me."

"I took all Sam's dog food, bowls, brushes, collar and a cash donation to the SPCA in her memory," wrote Maureen O. of California. "My boyfriend asked, 'Why did you do that? You can use them for your next dog.' He just didn't understand that these things were Sam's, and no other dog of mine could use them. Sam would have wanted them to go to an SPCA puppy or dog who really needed them, someone special because Sam was special."

There is no single right answer or best method for coping, however. Rosemary S. of California gave a convincing argument for *not* disposing of a pet's belongings!

"Getting rid of pictures, collars, toys, etc., right after the animal's death is not wise," she wrote. "You punish yourself by removing the very thing that brought you joy. I would often pick up a collar, toy or leash and remember walks we had, playful moments and so forth. It kept me in touch with a good memory, not the vague ones you might have if you eradicated all tangible evidence of the animal. We gave our next dog our deceased dog's collar, leash and toys, and we feel it has helped."

2. Change your schedule. Jamie Quackenbush, who worked for many years as a pet bereavement counselor at the University of Pennsylvania, noted that a pet owner often experiences strong feelings of depression at the times of the day when he or she was accustomed to interacting with the departed pet. If you had only one pet, for example, feeding time might be a painful focus for you. If you fed your pet regularly at 5 pm, you might feel a surge of emptiness and grief when 5 o'clock rolls around and you are forcibly reminded that you no longer have any reason to perform a routine that's virtually become part of you over the years. If you and your dog went on a long, companionable walk every morning at dawn, you might find that walking without your dog only makes you unhappy—but that avoiding the walks altogether only gives you time to sit and dwell on your loss.

It is at these moments—not the long hours of the day you spend at work or in other activities that didn't involve your pet while it was alive—that keep you aware of the hole the loss of your pet created in your life. Not only did the loss create a physical hole in your environment, it also created a hole in your normal activities and schedule.

If you find these "reminder" periods difficult to cope with, the only solution is to find ways to alter your schedule and fill the holes. Find something to occupy yourself with at 5 pm that won't take you into the kitchen; take a shower, work in the garden, take a walk, straighten the living room. Instead of telling yourself, "Now is the time I would have been feeding Precious," tell yourself, "Now is the time for my shower" or "my walk." Focus on the substitute activity, and make sure you've selected something that you enjoy doing, so that you can look forward to this time of day with anticipation rather than dread.

Instead of moping around the house when it is time for your dawn walk, find a friend to walk with and choose a new route. Or, use this time to read the morning paper, write letters, or perhaps write a journal about your life with your pet. If the "reminder period" is causing you to review old memories and sorrows, use it constructively by filling it with one of the strategies described below. You can choose to concentrate either on happy activities to distract you, or on a method of catharsis that will help you work through your grief at a time when it is most on your mind. Your choice may depend on where you are in the bereavement process, and what you feel you can handle at this time.

3. Write down your memories. It was difficult to decide whether this strategy belonged in the category of coping with emotions or adjusting to your pet's absence; indeed, it can be helpful for both. From what pet owners have said about recording their feelings, memories and experiences, however, it seems that this action does, in a way, help fill the hole caused by the pet's absence. Perhaps it creates a physical reminder of the pet that you can look at, read and reexperience, a reminder that keeps your pet alive in your heart and shows you that you can never really lose something you love. Such a reminder keeps your mind focused on the positive memories of your pet: If you find yourself missing it, you can read the account of your happy times together and turn sad feelings into happy memories. At the same time, writing down your memories serves as a catharsis for your emotions, a way to express them and work through them in private, on your own time, while creating a lasting memorial to a loved one.

"Besides crying, screaming and feeling all there was to feel, the thing that helped second-most was a written memorial," said Sue K. "I thought about what Titsie was really like: his quirks, his loves, his hates, and what he merely tolerated. I added a written and permanent reminder to my memory of the very special personality of my friend. I look at it now and it makes me smile."

One anonymous writer said that a professional counselor had suggested that she keep a journal of her feelings for one or two weeks. In later sessions, the owner brought the journal and pictures of her dog, which she and the counselor discussed. "It was painful but so helpful," wrote this owner. "I would definitely recommend pictures and a journal to anyone who loses a pet." Several pet owners also sent me copies of poems they had written in tribute to a departed pet.

Another pet owner wrote a "thank you letter" to her pet, listing all the things about the pet that had brought her happiness. When she felt sad, reading the letter would help her "enjoy" the pet again and make her feel better. Dr. Marcia Hutchinson suggests that owners "write an ongoing letter to their pets. Include in the letter any unresolved feelings (such as guilt), expressions of love, gratitude, making amends for behavior that was less than ideal, recollections of shared moments, and so forth." Counselor Maurine J. Sauters suggests, "in the writing of letters to pets, include 'words you wish you had said,' 'words you wish you had not said,' 'things you want to say you're sorry for,' and 'things you wish you had done'."

4. Create a memorial. Just as a written tribute gives you a tangible reminder of your pet that you can review whenever you feel the emptiness of its loss, a physical memorial of some kind gives you a visual reminder that may be helpful.

Photo memorials are a good way to commemorate a pet. "A day or two after each dog had died, I spent several hours going through my box of the pictures taken during their 17 years with me," wrote Helen B. of New York. "I selected all my favorites—ones that reflected good times and special aspects of their personalities—and took the negatives to have reprints and enlargements made. Then I made collages to put on the wall. Being able to see them like this every day makes their presence still a visible part of my life."

"When my puppy died, I found it helpful to go through my photo album and look at pictures of her," wrote Katie K. "Oh, it hurt a lot, but somehow the grief poured out of me through tears and it helped cleanse me. It also helped me remember what an important part of my life Bailey was, and how much different my life had been because of her."

Some pet owners who have chosen cremation for the remains of their pets have incorporated the urn containing the pet's ashes into a memorial. Today's pet urns have gone far beyond the traditional ginger-jar style: Urns are now available in a host of shapes and sizes and in fine woods, engraved metals, stone or stained glass, among other materials. You can order an urn that includes a portrait of your pet, an appropriate saying or epitaph, or whatever you desire. One pet owner wrote that her pet's ashes were in an urn that now sits on her television, wrapped in the pet's sweater; another flanked the urn with photos of the pet as a memorial that stands on her bookshelf.

"I suggest options for memorials that people usually haven't considered," says Betty Carmack, bereavement counselor for the San Francisco SPCA. She recommends such memorials as "a flowering bush or tree or plant in the animal's memory; a donation to an animal organization or to a human/animal program, group or department within a university; or a celebration or service in which others who knew the pet are invited to share in celebrating the pet's life and how that life touched their own."

When my cat Sebell died, I combined my love of cats with a love of shopping and spent a considerable sum of money at a shop that specialized in cat-motif products. A large part of this sum went to a bronze, almost life-size and very lifelike cat statue that I purchased specifically as a memorial to Sebell. In the weeks that followed his death, whenever I found myself looking at one of Sebell's favorite spots, I would look at the statue instead and concentrate on happy memories. Now the statue remains as a pleasant reminder of the love I had for this special pet. At the same shop, I purchased a needle-point kit that resembled a elderly cat belonging to my inlaws. When that cat, Emir, died, I was able to present them with the completed, framed piece of embroidery. This helped not only as a memorial, but to jar loose some needed tears that my inlaws had repressed for several months.

5. Help others. "It helped me to put all my spare time into helping find homes for stray animals," wrote one pet owner, who joined a volunteer organization dedicated to this task. Another, to ease her grief and to have contact with animals during the period when she still felt emotionally unable to adopt a new pet, acted as a foster parent for pets at a local animal shelter, and spent time at the shelter playing with some of the unwanted, unloved animals there. A bird owner wrote that he had put his energy into organizing a local bird club in the memory of his departed pet. Others wrote that donating to a pet-related charity helped ease their pain.

6. Concentrate on surviving pets. Obviously, if the pet you lost was your only pet, this coping strategy will not work for you. But if you have more than one pet, you may find that the survivors are of great help and comfort to you right now.

"Because our other two dogs were with me, I knew part of our little lost pet was still here," wrote Eva D. of Arizona. "Because of these beloved dogs, I had courage, and knew I still had their needs to take care of. Because of them, I could deal better with the loss of our little girl. The tears still come, but when they do, I get a lot of extra love and comfort from Rags and Pepper."

"Having other dogs in the house helped because the house felt less lonely," wrote Patricia B. of Ohio. "With only one dog, the house would have been empty."

"Did other pets help?" wrote Kathy D. of Oklahoma. "Not only does the need to take care of the other pets and to help them deal with the loss (perhaps even a greater loss to them than to us) help one deal with the grief and move on, but also one is not suddenly deprived of all the powerful benefits of companion animals. My pets missed her and looked for her and turned to me. Also, a second pet got distemper, and nursing her brought us closer. I'm sure this helped me overcome the grief and guilt feelings over the death of the other pet."

"It helped me to have other pets at the time of my loss because they had known the deceased also," wrote Pat H. of Pennsylvania. "I felt that there was a link between the animal I had lost and the animals that remained. It gave me great comfort to hold and hug all those furry bodies and just cry until I felt better. And it gave me great satisfaction to look at their strong, healthy bodies and sweet faces and to know that they, at least, would be with me for a while longer."

Some pet owners wrote that the presence of other animals did not help them much, however. Nancy P. of Washington wrote, "The dog that died was my 'baby.' Without his puppy antics, the house was unbearably quiet. What really distressed me about the other two dogs was their total lack of reaction to Sultan's death. I'd had no idea Sultan would go first; losing the most active part of the family left a void in the house I could not stand."

Other pet owners found little consolation in the survival of pets of a different type—for example, several wrote that their cats could not make up for the emptiness they felt over the loss of a dog. One wrote that the surviving pet was no comfort because it was a chicken. Some said that they found themselves resenting surviving pets for still being alive and healthy when a loved one had died. In general, however, it seems that having more than one pet at a time can be a great help in easing the pain of pet loss.

7. Get another pet. This was a frequent suggestion of pet owners. However, most agreed that if you have recently lost a pet, it is not a good idea to rush right out and buy another one. It's important to give yourself time to recover from your grief; otherwise, you may find yourself resenting the new pet, or expect it to be a carbon copy of the departed one. The decision to replace a pet should be made with care, and this topic will be discussed in greater detail in Chapter Five.

Will these coping strategies help? Can you recover and go on with a normal life and love new pets? If your grief is fresh in your mind, you may feel right now that the answer is no. But Minta of Texas has another view.

"Since my husband is now 60 years old, and I am only five years behind him, and since we have always had pets, there have been more than just one death to contend with over the years. We've loved each of them, we've cried over their loss, and we've deeply missed each of them as they left us. Still, we will always have pets, and we will face the same heartbreak of loss over again.

"We feel that we had the love to give the ones we lost and still have that love to offer, so why deny it to one who is alive and in need of it? Our rewards are far greater than theirs, and our lives are far richer for having been shared with our dogs and cats... even for a little while.

"We don't forget the departed ones—we frequently talk about the 'remember whens'—but we don't dwell on our losses. We continue to build new memories with newfound furry friends. When they are gone, one misses them, but life goes on. One must put aside the deep depression of loss and continue to live with the fond memories—while loving others."

Chapter 4

A Family Affair

IF YOU'RE ONE OF THE MANY PET OWNERS in this country who live alone, you may be the only person to be strongly affected by the death of your pet. Though your relatives and friends may be understanding and sympathetic, they may not fully share your grief. True grief is the province of those who have lived with and loved a pet day in and day out, not of those who had only a casual acquaintance with it.

In a family, however, every member—spouse, children, parents, even other pets—is deeply affected by the loss of a pet. In addition, different family members may have had different types of relationships with the pet, and may experience grief at different levels and in different ways. As Carol F. of Kentucky writes, "The entire family grieved over Chadwick's death. He had been something very special to each of us, and something different to each of us. He had been my companion, my friend, my confidante, many times my lifeline in times of trouble. To my husband, he offered unqualified love and acceptance, which had immeasurable value. To our daughter, he was a little brother."

Communication is the most powerful tool a family has for dealing with the loss of a pet. Nothing hinders recovery from grief so much as a house full of people who are trying to hide their pain from one another, who are refusing to accept their own pain, or who are reacting negatively and critically to the pain of others.

All too often, however, this is precisely what happens. Families frequently get trapped in role-playing. Parents, for example, may cling to the notion that it is important for them to appear calm and unmoved, no matter what happens; they believe that this is how they bring security and stability to the family. They may fear that if they seem upset or "fall apart," their children will become upset or frightened. Thus many parents attempt to maintain the illusion that "all is well," no matter how deeply they are hurting.

This often gives children the idea that Mom and Dad *aren't* hurt by the loss of the pet—and that, therefore, Mom and Dad really didn't care that much about the pet in the first place. A child may then attempt to conceal his own grief, fearing that his parents won't understand or will dismiss it as childish and silly. Or, children may attempt to emulate their parents' example of false strength, concealing their grief in an effort to appear "adult" about the matter. They may suppose that "big kids" don't cry about the death of a pet, that grief is something only for the immature and weak. The entire household may end up suffering in misunderstood silence.

"I've had many clients whose spouse tries to get them to hold in their feelings and 'not cry in front of the children,'" says counselor Maryann Borgon. "I encourage clients to talk honestly to their children, and if they are sad, to cry. This shows the children that it's okay to express emotion at the death of a pet, and later this will reflect on how they cope and react to a human death. I also urge people to include children in ceremonies that will add closure to the death (a burial service, writing or sharing stories about the pet, planting a memorial tree or flower). I tell parents to share their feelings and ask their children if they want to talk about theirs; this open discussion shows children that 'it's okay' and that they won't be judged or ridiculed."

Sex roles can also make grieving difficult. A husband and father may attempt to maintain the role of "strong, silent pillar of the family." He may believe that, even though everyone else is crying and carrying on, *he* must keep up an illusion of strength, or his family will lose confidence in him. Many men have been taught from childhood that loving a pet is the sort of slushy sentimentality appropriate only for women and children: A "real" man shouldn't let himself get all choked up over an animal! Thus, even when a man cares deeply for a pet, he may find it very uncomfortable to express his feelings of loss and sorrow—or may not even know how!

"I have had several male clients who experienced a great deal of difficulty expressing grief," writes counselor Sandra Barker, Ph.D. "Men raised in 'traditional' homes where male emotional expression was discouraged often have a great deal of concern about not being able to 'control' their intense feelings over the pet's death. Many think that they have to be the strong one in the family, and they equate strength with not expressing painful emotions. Such men endure much suffering in silence."

"A common request from my male clients is, 'Isn't there a shortcut to get through this grief quickly?' " says Borgon. "Several of my clients got very angry at their wives because the wives expressed their grief and the husbands 'didn't know how' or were 'too embarrassed' to let the pain out. They'd say hurtful things to family members. I explain that sometimes we do these things to try to ease our own hurt because we don't know what to do, but we end up hurting those we love."

A wife and mother may wish to avoid appearing weak or "overemotional" in front of her husband and children. She, too, may believe that grieving over a pet is a sign of feminine sentimentality and weakness—especially if her husband thinks so (or appears to think so) as well! She may suppose that, as a mature adult, she should be stronger, "above" such emotions. If her husband is not displaying grief, she may be embarrassed to reveal the depth of her own reactions, fearful that he does not share or understand her feelings—or worse, as Maryann Borgon pointed out, that he will react with anger, condemnation, or harsh words.

A husband can inadvertently encourage this type of emotional repression by complimenting his wife on "how well" she is handling the loss. Not being psychic, he may assume that because she is not displaying sorrow and pain, she isn't feeling any. He might be very willing to offer comfort if he knew that it was needed—but if the wife isn't being honest about her feelings, the husband may never know that she needs his support. This can create some very tense feelings in the household, as each family member tries to respond to the feelings he or she *thinks* the other family members have, rather than the feelings they *actually* have.

The end result of this kind of situation is not only a lot of unresolved pain and grief in a family, but also a lot of unresolved anger. If you hurt and no one seems to care, or you can't express your hurt, or you wish that you *didn't* hurt and you don't want to think about it, you're going to start to feel angry. If you don't want to be reminded of your pain (a common issue for men), anything that forces you to think about that pain is likely to make you angry. This is why many men react angrily or critically toward the grief of other family members. It is not that they are angry that the other person is grieving; it is because that person's grief is calling their attention to feelings that they may wish they didn't have or that they could more easily control.

A wife who can't find comfort and understanding for her feelings may start to feel resentment toward her "unsympathetic" or "uncaring" husband, and this anger will emerge at unexpected times, often over petty matters that have nothing to do with the pet. Children who see their parents as uncaring and unsympathetic will also often exhibit anger or moodiness. This, in turn, often provokes an angry response from the parents, who find that moody kids are the last thing they want to cope with in the midst of all this. Before long, all these unresolved emotions start spiraling out of control.

Sharing the Healing

To avoid these difficulties, which only complicate and compound the pain everyone is already feeling over the loss of a beloved pet, it is vital to share the grieving process as a family. When the grief is shared and discussed, the loss of a pet can actually help bring a family closer together instead of driving it farther apart—but for this to happen, the ability (and willingness) to communicate openly, honestly, and nonjudgmentally is vital.

"Don't try to conceal grief behind a macho mask," urges Muriel Franzblau of the Bide-a-Wee Home Association. "Be actively one of the bereaved rather than a tower of strength. This will help your family through this sad time; otherwise, hostility is created because you appear indifferent and uncaring. Unexpressed grief wreaks havoc in men as well as women and children. Be very gentle with them and with yourself. Share the mourning process fully."

"I always encourage hugging between spouses, especially when words don't come easily," says Maryann Borgon. "I'll tell them to just say, 'I need a hug now, I'm really hurting.' That closeness helps couples cope together."

C. Miriam Yarden has a suggestion for men who aren't sure how to deal with their grief: "I ask a man to consider the fact that, in the area of feelings, they are not one bit different from women. And indeed, why should they be? Without the full gamut of emotions, something would be missing. Why should sorrow and pain, tenderness and tears, be the exclusive property of women? These feelings are much too precious to deny. The man usually comes to the conclusion that he has as much right to feel pain as anyone, and that being strong and tough and unemotional leaves him somehow incomplete. And, as long as he has the feelings, he has the same right (and obligation to himself) to express them. He also concludes that if anyone else has a problem with that, it is their problem rather than his.

"It's not as easy as it sounds," she adds. "Too many men are so deeply conditioned that they will deny, ignore, or bury the hurt too deeply. When it does work and there is a breakthrough, however, there is also great relief and renewal."

Yarden suggests a family counsel as a way to begin breaking down the barriers that are isolating family members from one another. Bringing everyone together, so that everyone can discover that their feelings are shared, is a tremendous step toward family healing.

"When my mother died," Yarden writes, "everybody mourned separately. I mourned for the loss of a mother, my daughter mourned for the loss of her grandmother—everyone mourned in a different way. Finally I called them all together to talk about it and mourn together. 'Let's cry,' I said, 'let's remember, let's talk about it.' It was the most painful, most wonderful, agonizing half day we ever spent, but it worked. Everyone was crying, and it created support; no one found it weakening or enfeebling."

If your household is suffering from lack of communication, you might want to try the same procedure. Since you have chosen to read this book, you have clearly been able to acknowledge your own grief and the need to find a way to work through it. It may be up to you to help the rest of your family take the same step.

For a family counsel to work, you need to set aside a period when no one has time limits to be concerned about, and when everyone is fresh. A weekend is often the best time; no one has to go to work or school, and no one is exhausted from having worked or studied all day. Take the phone off the hook and don't answer the door. Try what Yarden tried: Be honest, tell your family what you need to talk about, and why. Make it clear that this is not a place for judgments or ridicule; this is a time for honesty and sharing, for crying without shame, for remembering pain and remembering good times as well.

One device Yarden uses in her grief counseling sessions is to ask her client to "tell me about Precious," from the birth of the pet to its death. The story usually "starts with difficulty," Yarden says, "but then it spills out. It slows down when it gets to the bad times," such as the pet's final illness, but Yarden takes the client through the steps of the illness or the accident, to the very end. This method works well in helping a client see that his or her feelings of guilt and anger often have no foundation in reality, and provide a more realistic perspective on the pet's death and the client's involvement in it.

You might want to try the same approach, or ask each family member what they remember in particular about the pet. For one it might be the morning romps through the dewy grass in the park, for another the whispered confidences at night in bed, where the dog wasn't supposed to be (don't, regardless of your parental urges, choose this time to scold the child who smuggled the dog into the bedroom!). You might recall how the dog trusted you when it was sick or helpless, or how you felt when you brought home the puppy—your frustration when it chewed up your best purse and wet the carpet, mixed with your steadily growing love for the creature. You might want to help encourage memories by going over photos of the pet.

This may provide you with an opportunity to help yourself and your family work through the reactions described in Chapter Two. You may discover, for example, that everyone in the family has feelings of guilt over the pet's death: your child because he let the dog out that day without making sure the gate was closed, your husband for not closing the gate, you for not checking the yard more often. One family member may be angry at the veterinarian for letting the pet die, another at the accident that sent the pet to the hospital in the first place, and yet another at the pet for being stupid enough to run in front of that car. By bringing these different issues of guilt and blame into the open, you and your family may be able to realize that there was no single cause of death to blame, no single person responsible, and that these individual feelings have no basis in reality but are simply getting in the way of the healing process.

Never force a meeting on a family member, however. It is possible that a member of your family really didn't care much about the family pet, and does not have anything to contribute or to gain from this type of meeting. Or, more probably, a family member may still be having too much difficulty coming to terms with grief to handle this potentially painful and revealing experience. In grieving, as with all things, you can knock on the door, but you can't force an entry. Each grieving person must make the choice to open the door and seek help, or to keep it closed and find alternate ways of dealing with the situation.

Helping Children Cope

Pets and children seem to just naturally go together. Researchers who study child behavior and development have come up with a number of complicated explanations for the reasons children and pets mesh so beautifully. They speak of the numerous benefits children derive from this relationship, including an understanding of responsibility, interpersonal interactions, communication and more.

Those of us who grew up with pets understand this relationship in more simple terms. We remember how pets never teased us or mocked our blunders or sorrows, and how we could confide our secrets to them in complete safety. If we were imaginative, we may have turned our pets into any number of companions: heroes, wild Kiplingesque wolves or tigers that only we Mowglis could tame, ferocious beasts to conquer in mock-battles, or faithful sidekicks to rescue us from hordes of imaginary enemies. Pets were our allies against the world, friends who were always on our side when parents picked on us, siblings harassed us, human friends abandoned us and bullies made our lives miserable. Those of us who remember times like these know how devastating the loss of a pet can be to our own children.

Carol F. knew how much her poodle, Chadwick, meant to her daughter, Melanie. "He was her little brother. She was less than 2 years old when we adopted Chadwick, so she could not even remember life without him. He had been her playmate, her baby brother that never grew up. In some ways his death hit her the hardest."

Carol found that Melanie reacted just as strongly to unfeeling comments from others as an adult pet owner might. "One day shortly after Chadwick died, we met someone in the grocery store who we thought would care, and told her about his death. I don't remember who it was or what she said, but Melanie needed to leave in a hurry after that. When we got in the car she said, 'Mom, she thinks Chadwick was just a dog...' Of course he was a dog, but to us he was so much more, and some people just did not comprehend that."

To make matters worse, the death of a family pet may be a child's first encounter with death, so that a parent is faced not only with trying to soothe the child's grief over the disappearance of a friend, but with trying to explain the *concept* of death. This can prove no easy task, since few adults have a ready explanation of death at hand even for themselves. Television, one of a child's primary sources of information these days, is little help at all, when cartoon characters survive all manner of violent acts and characters killed off at the end of one season can be miraculously resurrected at the beginning of the next. How does one explain to a child what happened to a pet, and why it won't come home again?

As in all things related to dealing with grief in the family, communication is the key. It's a good idea not to make assumptions about what your child does or does not understand, or what beliefs your child may hold. Television isn't the only source of information children have. Children receive input from a wide range of sources over which you have no control, including books, magazines, radio, records, other children, teachers, and other adults.

Information from these sources may be filtered through the child's own experiences (some of which you may know nothing about, no matter how observant you are), his or her personal values and family values, and by whatever other interpretation and sorting processes go on in a young brain. By talking to your child openly and honestly (which means sharing your own feelings), you may find that the child understands death far better than you anticipated, or you may be able to uncover some misconceptions that you now have an opportunity to put right.

Children of different ages may react differently to a pet's death. In addition, children of different ages tend to have different types of relationships with a pet. While a pet may seem like a cuddly plaything to a toddler, it may seem like a furry sibling and confidante to an older child, and a source of continuity and love to a teenager. Certainly, the older a child grows, the more experiences are shared, and the stronger the sense of companionship grows. Very soon, the pet ceases to be an interesting furry toy and becomes a distinct personality to a child, perceived as capable of understanding and sharing.

You may discover, by watching your pets and children interact, that the pets themselves establish these dividing lines in the relationship. An adult dog, for instance, may regard a baby or toddler rather like a puppy, something that may need watching and guarding, but not something that one romps with as an equal. Cats will often stay well out of reach of young children who haven't learned to be gentle or respectful yet. But as the child grows older and is more able to understand how to interact with pets, the boundaries between them tend to come down.

Counselor Diane Matheny has a suggestion for helping younger children cope with the loss of a pet. "I find it helpful to have them tell me where they think their pet is now. I encourage them to describe the setting, the other animals or people they believe would be there, and what their pet does for fun. Through this creative exercise, I can find out if there are aspects of death that are frightening to the child, and address them. While children may initially have a rather vague idea of the afterlife of the pet, they enjoy exploring the possibilities. Imagination is a big part of a child's life, and this exercise can be a helpful way to introduce information and ease fears when a child loses a pet.

"I am comfortable telling children that no one knows for sure where we go when we die. Honesty is essential when dealing with children, and since we don't know exactly where we go when we die, it is important to tell them that, too. When the family has a spiritual or religious background, I integrate these beliefs in the exercise. Generally, once a child has visualized where the pet might be, feels sure that the pet's needs are met, and realizes that the pet will not awaken in its grave, he can move on to the acceptance stage of grieving."

Though some counselors believe that teenagers are less likely to grieve deeply over the loss of a pet, Matheny disagrees. "I personally feel that the relationship between a teenager and his or her pet can be far closer than we realize," she says. "I still use some of the visualization techniques mentioned above for this age group. There is a good possibility that many teenagers have bonded very closely with their pets, in light of the less traditional family structures our culture has produced. When a teenager loses an animal, she may have lost the only companion who was always there for her.

"I feel that it is important to encourage the child to explore her current support system, and possibly to advise her how to find someone else who can be there through this difficult period. This age group seems to find comfort from an older adult friend who can listen, offer suggestions, and provide nurturing. Teens often find it difficult to show their vulnerable feelings to peers, who might not understand and who are often unable to answer questions about death and loss.

"With this age group, I use the technique of memorializing the pet by suggesting that the teenager choose one of the animal's endearing qualities and manifesting it in her daily life. For example, if the teenager loved the way her cat always greeted her in a warm manner, she could begin to express more warmth when she greets people. Frequently, people mention unconditional love or being a good listener as their favorite qualities in animals. By behaving in these ways ourselves, we can keep the memory of our pets alive while honoring the benefits of our relationship with them."

The story Regina S. of Pennsylvania tells about the death of her family dog, Queenie, demonstrates not only how much a dog can mean to a teenager, but how important family communication and openness are in dealing with pet loss. Regina was 13 when Queenie, 8, was diagnosed as having cancer and had to be euthanized. Her account, written six years later, shows how deeply sensitive a child may be not only to her own reactions, but to those of other family members.

"I remember driving to the SPCA with Queenie between my parents on the front seat," wrote Regina. "The three kids were in the back seat. I remember thinking to myself that maybe we would get lost and go back home so Queenie wouldn't have to be put to sleep. But we didn't get lost, and arrived at the SPCA sooner than I wanted to. We all took Queenie in and handed her to a man who took her down the hall as we were watching. Before Queenie went into the room, she looked back at us as if to say good-bye. My mom burst out crying and so did I. We hugged each other because we knew we both felt the same pain of seeing our pet hurt as badly as she did. My dad, brother and sister all had tears filling their eyes also.

"After that day, if I saw a picture of Queenie or heard a slow song that reminded me of her, I would start crying again. My family was very helpful to me. My mom would tell me that Queenie had been in pain and now she was at rest. It really helped to know I had my family to depend on.

"A month later my parents went to the SPCA and picked out a beautiful black and white miniature Collie/Beagle. At first I didn't want this cute puppy, whom we named King, because I still wanted Queenie. But as days went by I seemed to love King. Now that little bundle of joy is 6 years old. King is truly my dog and the love and care I give him don't match the great love he gives me in return."

Some people say that one should never use the term "went to sleep" in connection with death, or a child may develop a fear of going to sleep because he is afraid that, like Fido, he won't wake up. They also argue that if you say that the pet was so sick or so badly injured that it went to sleep or went to heaven, the child may fear that this may happen to him if he becomes sick or injured. The child may also fear that if this could happen to the family dog, it could also happen to someone else in the family, like Mommy or Daddy.

Yarden doesn't hesitate to use this expression, however, and it is extremely likely that your child is bound to hear it anyway. "Going to sleep" seems to be our most common euphemism for death, both human and animal, and if your child doesn't hear it from you, he will probably hear it from another child, another adult, a veterinarian or perhaps a doctor. You may need to expand your explanation and point out the difference between sick and very, very sick; between a sprained ankle and a very serious injury. You may also wish to explain that dogs and cats get old much faster than humans do, and that 15 years for a pet is a long life while 15 years for a child is a very short time.

As for the child's fears that what happened to his pet might also happen to him, or to his parents or siblings, let's be honest with ourselves: it might. None of us are immortal, and accident, illness or old age could strike a family member at any time. While your first purpose in explaining a pet's death to a young child is to soothe the child's fears, it may be unwise to try to banish those fears by making promises that in reality you have little control over. The death of a pet can be one way for anyone of any age to come to grips with an understanding of our own mortality.

Never tell your child anything that will imply that the child was at fault, or that the separation isn't permanent. Statements such as "he went away" or "he didn't like it here anymore, so he left," leave a child with unnecessary confusion and guilt. Did the pet go away, the child may wonder, because I pulled its tail or yelled at it? Is it my fault? Might it come back if I promised to be a nice person? If the child does not understand that the pet can never come back, he may be reluctant to accept another pet, but be determined to wait loyally for the departed one's return.

If your pet is sick and you know that it is bound to die in

the near future, you will do your child more good by preparing him for this inevitable tragedy than by trying to conceal the pet's condition. This way, your child will be able to observe the pet's illness and develop a better understanding of the dying process.

"We adopted a dog, Clifford, from a shelter a year ago," wrote Susan K. of New York. "Six months ago, he was diagnosed as having severe kidney damage. The disease is progressing and we must prepare for his eventual death. He and my 4-year-old daughter are best friends. I've prepared her by explaining that he is sick and may die someday. We have read children's books from the library dealing with a pet's death." Susan is also preparing herself during this process, both by explaining the situation to her daughter and by learning as much as she can about her dog's condition so that she can monitor it. "Having lost a pet before enables me to be honest with myself that it will hurt a lot when he's gone."

You can serve your children best by being as honest as possible about the death of the pet, or about an illness that will eventually lead to death. Honesty and openness will pave the way to coping, and will enable you and your children to have discussions about your feelings. If you fail to be open, your children may hear things from other sources that give them confused ideas about what has happened, and without communication you'll have no opportunity to learn what these ideas are or how to counteract them.

Four-Legged Family Members

You've probably noticed that your pets react to any type of change in your household. If you move a piece of furniture, or remove one, or add something new, your pets may carefully investigate the change, check out the box the new furniture came in, perhaps claim new territory for their own, perhaps express displeasure—but you can be sure they'll *notice*. Pets also notice when a family member, human or animal, is missing. I once got a severe scolding from my cats when I returned from dinner several hours after my husband; the cats had seen us leave together, and in their experience, we should have come home together. They were greatly concerned by the change in our normal routine.

It is small wonder, then, that pets often seem to react to the loss of another pet. These reactions range from what seems to be mild concern to apparent deep depression; in more than one instance, a pet owner wrote that she was concerned about the way the surviving pet's emotional reactions were affecting its physical health. While many animal behaviorists advise pet owners not to "anthropomorphize" their pets and attribute human emotions to them, it is difficult to interpret the reactions of some pets as anything other than grief over the disappearance of a companion.

"Most of my pets choose a 'special friend' from the menagerie, and when one of the pair dies, the remaining friend seems especially saddened," wrote Pat H. of Pennsylvania. "When we lost our Old English Sheepdog, Brendan, to cancer, our other Sheepdog, Dulcie, became severely depressed. All she wanted to do was eat and sleep. We showered her with extra attention and love, but it didn't help. She showed no interest in our other pets, either.

"We solved the problem by going to our local shelter and adopting a lively puppy for Dulcie. No one can be depressed (or sleep) with a yappy, biting, distracting and irritating puppy crawling all over her! Dulcie decided that someone had to take this youngster in hand and teach him some manners. With renewed interest in life, she applied herself to the task! Our new puppy captured Dulcie's heart, and ours as well."

"When Captain was put to sleep, his brother, Freddie, was devastated," wrote Karen L. of North Carolina. "He looked everywhere—in closets, cabinets, etc.—for his brother. He refused to play and ate very little. He just wanted me to hold him. One night he curled up next to me and actually cried, which, of course, broke my heart.

"Since Freddie had seen his daddy carry Captain out and then come home again without him, he refused to go anywhere, even out in the yard, alone with my husband. Only in the past six months has Freddie regained trust in his daddy."

"We observed an unusual reaction from our Keeshond in response to the death of one of our two cats," wrote Marie S. of Pennsylvania. "Rip suddenly started giving an occasional funny bark and having a mild seizure. The vet diagnosed it as epilepsy and prescribed medication.

"Two or three months later, the family was viewing old slide pictures, and a picture of Willow, the deceased cat, came on the screen. Rip got excited and ran to the screen, and then cried and searched behind the screen for the cat. Then we realized how much Rip missed 'Pussy Willow the Little Dickens.' We stopped using her name in conversation, and of course, didn't show any more pictures.

"We also recalled that Rip had stayed right by Willow when she was ill, and that the seizures had begun after her death. We consulted the vet about the possibility of Rip's spells being psychological. He suggested stopping the medication. If it were psychological, the spells would stop; if it were epilepsy, they would continue. Well, it's been years now and Rip has never shown the symptoms again!"

"Our 10-year-old male dog, Corby, and his 13-year-old mother were very close," wrote Evelyn S. of West Virginia. "Corby went into a deep depression after his mother died. He refused to eat or drink. Only with the aid of medication were we able to save him. He lost five pounds before we got him out of it. He didn't look for her around the house because he knew she wasn't there. He lay around and grieved. His bed was beside the wall in our bedroom, and Lisa's had been in the corner of the same room. We removed her bed and he would stand and look at the spot for long periods of time. Finally, after about six months, he began sleeping in her spot and we put his bed there. That was 18 months ago, and he still sleeps in her spot.

"Taking such care of Corby, trying to keep him alive, helped assuage our own grief. Attention to him took all our time. He is now back to his happy-go-lucky self."

Not every pet owner observed grief-like reactions in surviving pets. In Chapter Three, Nancy P. expressed her anger at the lack of reaction displayed by two of her dogs over the death of the third. But, as she wrote, "The three dogs were never very close anyway." That may provide the key: The more attached pets are to one another, the more likely they will be to miss one another. This closeness goes beyond species lines; as these letters indicated, dogs mourn for cats, and I've seen cats mope after the death of a favorite dog.

If a relationship between two pets seems stressful for one

of them—for instance, if the dominant cat constantly beats up on a subordinate cat—you might expect the "victimized" survivor to be relieved at the loss of the dominant pet. After years of being driven off chairs and beds by her overbearing brother, we thought our surviving cat would not miss him much when he died, and might take the opportunity to become more assertive. Instead, she lay listlessly on the sofa, staring into space, seeming to have little interest in living. So we brought home a new cat, and the survivor, now "top cat," seems quite happy driving the newcomer off chairs and beds.

Since pets react much like other family members, part of your task in helping your family cope with the loss of a pet may well include giving comfort and support to a surviving pet. Obviously, you can't do this by having open and honest discussions of feelings with a pet—though a one-sided conversation of this type certainly won't do your pet any harm, and may even do you some good. Extra attention, distractions in the form of walks and play sessions, treats, and sometimes some very special care may be called for to help your pet cope with the loss of a friend.

Sometimes the introduction of a new pet is the one thing that brings a surviving pet—or any other family member—out of its mourning and depression. You may even find, as we did, that the needs of your remaining pet are what drive you to "replace" your lost animal. But bringing a new pet into your home isn't always as easy as it sounds. The next chapter will discuss the steps one should take and things one should think about before obtaining a new pet.

No matter what the size, shape and structure of your family unit—traditional, nontraditional, blended, whatever—the important thing to remember is that the loss of one member of this unit affects everyone, including your other pets. It is also important to remember that the loss may affect every family member in a different way, which is why communication is so important.

Communication prevents us from making false assumptions about how other family members feel, either based on how we ourselves are feeling, or on how we interpret the reactions of others. Communication helps us to understand that there is more than one way (and no one *right* way) to relate to a pet, and more than one way to respond to its loss. Finally, communication helps us come together and gain strength and comfort from one another in a time of loss, instead of becoming isolated and trapped in our grief. After all, we are grieving because we have lost someone we loved—and if nothing else, our pets have helped teach us the value of sharing love, support, comfort, and unconditional acceptance with one another!

Chapter 5

Welcoming A New Pet

L OSING A BELOVED PET can be like losing a part of
oneself. As you go through the pain, the depression,
the anger and the guilt, you may feel that this is too
terrible an experience to endure again. The one sure way to
avoid a repetition of this trauma is to decide never to own a
pet again.

"I felt at the time that I never wanted another pet or to
have to go through this again," wrote Georgetta G. of Arkansas. Jean-Irene of Illinois agreed: "Needless to say, I said that
I would *never* get another dog and have to go through 'that'
again."

Yet both Georgetta and Jean-Irene changed their minds,
and they, along with hundreds of other pet owners, offer this
piece of advice for coping with bereavement: "Get another pet."
This may seem like a bit of a paradox: "Why do so many of us
pet owners get more pets knowing that these, too, will eventually die and we will experience the same hurt as before?"
asks Mary K. of Minnesota, who writes that she will never be
without a dog. "Are we gluttons for punishment, or just basking in the joy of a pet to love?"

From what other pet owners write, "basking" seems to be

the answer. "All I can say about a pet's death," wrote Jean-Irene, "is that it is something we do not look forward to, but each pet is so precious and individual in personality, so it is our loss if we do not love and take care of these special creatures created by God. They give so much love and beauty and demand nothing of us except our love and care."

"Do not shy away from another pet because of the pain you feel now," wrote Gwen V. of New York. "There are many, many pets out there who need you, and after all, surely that short time of grief is well worth the many years of love a pet will give you!"

"I hurt so much for people who feel they cannot allow themselves to have another animal once that special pet is gone," wrote Barbara T. of New Jersey. "By sparing themselves the pain caused by losing a well-loved friend, they are cutting themselves off from so much. Getting a new pet really helps—just think of putting all those bits and pieces you learned from your old friend to use in training and getting to know a new one. It's not a replacement, it's an enhancement of the affection you felt for your previous pet."

C. Miriam Yarden believes that to decide you'll never get another pet is to deny the value of the first. "You're telling your dead pet that it wasn't good enough," she says. "The good times weren't enough to make up for the pain."

What Your Pet Would Want

One thing that often stands in the way of obtaining a new pet is a sense of loyalty. The deceased pet was a member of the family, and has a virtually sacred place in your heart and memory. "Obtaining" a new pet can become confused with "replacing" the old pet—and, you may think, no one could replace Precious. How could you even think of bringing a newcomer into your home, to let it take the place of Precious in your heart, to eat where Precious ate and sleep where Precious slept? It's a violation of your loved one's memory, an intrusion. After all, how can you replace a member of the family? No other pet could be like the one you lost.

This is absolutely true: No other pet *will* have the unique qualities of the pet you lost, nor should you expect it to. Problems often arise when a pet owner hopes that the new pet will be a replacement, a peg that will fit precisely into the hole left by the dead pet so that you will no longer have to face the emptiness. But just as no two family members are alike— even twin siblings—no two pets will be alike either. It is important to remember that every pet will have unique qualities of its own. Thus, instead of viewing a new pet as "replacement," try to think of it as making a new friend, one that you will learn about and come to love over time.

If a sense of loyalty to the departed pet is holding you back from bringing a new one into your home, think a moment about what your pet wanted from life. Dogs, for example, seem particularly interested in pleasing their owners, and owners both of dogs and of cats often comment on how sensitive their pets are to their moods. Pets don't want their owners to be unhappy. Barbara Y. of Delaware realized this shortly after her Welsh Corgi died.

"When I lost my Sheba," she wrote, "I felt as if a part of me had died too. My Corgi was my child. She was so loved by everyone.

"The week she died, we went to look for another Corgi. We found a little female that looked so much like Sheba. My husband just knew that was the puppy for us. I didn't want one. We went home and I cried for hours on end.

"Then I looked at Sheba's picture in my arms, and remembered how she always got upset when I was upset. She'd give me so many kisses if she thought something was wrong. Sheba would want me to open up my heart to another. I started thinking about all the love and happiness she brought to us. Back we went and got that little one like our Sheba.

"Now I look at Sheba's picture in our living room and smile. She'd be happy for me too. The only sorrow she ever gave me was on the day she left me. Getting another pet is the best thing in the world. It can never replace the one you lost in your heart, but it will make a place of its own."

Celia P. of New York had a similar experience. "What helped me accept my new pet the most was the realization that Cam would have wanted me to have another baby to love. I had awful days when I could not love that pup for her own sake, but I could love her because Cam would have. A phrase from the Bible kept going through my head: 'Accepted in the beloved.' I don't know what a theologian would think, but my little girl was loved for my beloved Cam's sake long before I could love her for herself."

"Why would you think loving another pet makes you love the first one(s) less?" asks Kathy D. of Oklahoma. "Can't you love more than one friend, more than one child? It's tragic when hurt people never have another pet. God gave them to us to help, not to hurt us. We have to open up and let ourselves heal."

When Is the Right Time?

Quite a few people believe that the best way to console oneself upon the death of a pet is to "get a new one right away." Most, however, are not experienced pet owners, but well-meaning friends or relatives.

When a friend's Poodle suffered an accident while staying with the friend's mother during the day, the mother rushed out to a pet store and bought another Poodle on the spot. My friend came home not only to discover that her dog was dead, but that there was a new dog in the house that she was expected to love right away. The parents were not pet owners and did not understand that pets are not interchangeable pieces of fur, or that one cannot instantly transfer one's affections from one to another. A pet is an individual with strengths and weaknesses, quirks and delights, just like any other individual that pet owner knows. Most pet owners I've spoken with agree that one needs time to mourn and come to terms with the death of the last pet before taking on the next one.

Rosemary S. of California saw what could happen if a pet owner didn't take this time to adjust to the loss. "My sister lost her cat to feline leukemia," she wrote. "She immediately got another—within a few weeks. She got a kitten, and ended up taking it back to the animal shelter in a few days. It was apparent she had not gone through any steps to accept, grieve, understand, and finalize the death and learn to go on."

A pet obtained too soon can cause resentment. Your emotions are too caught up in the process of coping with your loss to allow you to deal with establishing a new relationship smoothly. On the two occasions that my household has obtained a new pet within two or three weeks of the loss of a previous one—once when I was a teenager and once when I was an adult—I felt the same reaction: "I can't love you! I still love the other one. You aren't the pet I *want*, and you're here trying to take the love that I'm not ready to give to someone else." Yet pets that arrived after a longer interval aroused no such feelings of antagonism.

"I've gone both routes—getting another dog immediately and waiting a short time," wrote Gwen V. "I found it much easier to accept the new puppy knowing I had gotten used to the idea that my Clancy was gone. You need to have accepted the death of your treasured friend, or you run the risk of expecting the new addition to be a replacement, rather than a different identity. And this may take awhile. Don't try to kid yourself. It was more than a month before I could honestly say that I didn't look for my dog while at home, exercising, etc. I still cry as I write this! Only after I became comfortable being alone did I look for another dog. And, two weeks ago, my boyfriend surprised me with a beautiful little Cairn Terrier puppy, whom I adore!"

Sometimes the decision almost seems to be made for you, and you may find that you were more ready for it than you thought. Just as we adopted a kitten far sooner than we intended to because our surviving cat seemed so much in need of a companion, you may find that another member of your family prompts you to acquire a pet sooner than you might otherwise do so.

"I probably would not have gotten another dog, but my children, ages 6 and 10, saw a Springer Spaniel puppy and begged for one," wrote Jan R. of Tennessee. "We bought a liver-and-white female (Freckles had been a black-and-white male). We thought a different color would help the children accept her as an individual, not as a replacement. Freckles died last June and we brought Lily home at Thanksgiving. She has become a member of our family, but Freckles is still in our hearts and we miss him."

"I never intended to go through that again, but one of my daughters (our children are all married and gone now) talked me into going into a pet shop with her," said Rosemary T. of Texas. "They just happened to have Lhasa Apso puppies, and my daughter was sure I needed one. I wasn't so sure. But somehow I found myself taking one home. Tiger is 1-1/2 years old now and beautiful, and so sweet. I did have trouble adjusting to him at first and found myself comparing him to Priscilla without meaning to. But his care took so much of my time that the grief got easier each day."

How long should you wait before obtaining a new pet? Some pet owners have waited six months, some a year or more. But there is no "right" figure, no set amount of time for the bereavement process to take its course. What may take months for one person to resolve, another may handle in a matter of weeks or less. Different people may be more affected by different elements of grief. For example, while one person may be most affected by the resentment he or she feels toward a new pet, another may be more affected by the loneliness that the absence of the departed pet brings. While the first individual may find that a new pet acquired too soon makes the coping process more difficult, the second may find his coping hindered by the emptiness of a petless house.

"The silence in the house was deafening, and I thought I would go mad," wrote Deborah C. of Pennsylvania. "Her favorite napping place and her bed were like a knife in my heart. Three days later I could no longer stand the loneliness, and we got a 6-week-old Golden Retriever, Buffy. She can never take Patches' place in my heart, but she found a new place all her own. She's simply wonderful, and of course I love her just as much, just a little differently. Kitty didn't take to her right away, but after a few weeks they were loyal playmates."

"I was surprised when in less than a week I wanted to get another dog," wrote Joyce P. of Arizona, whose experience in looking for a new pet made her wonder a little about fate. "I had a terrible time after Muffin passed away. She had given me such immeasurable love. I looked in the newspaper and saw several dogs advertised for sale and some for free. I called several of the numbers but was told that most of the dogs were gone already. Then I called a kennel that had advertised an 8-month-old black Poodle. The owner was so kind that I found myself crying about Muffin's death. The owner said I sounded like the person for the little Poodle.

"I went to the kennel the next morning and was introduced to a precious little dog that was half-starved. Her owner had brought her back to the kennel because she wasn't living up to the owner's expectations, and the owner thought she would like another dog. The poor little thing was grieving. I took her home and my daughter and I named her Babette.

"I brought Babette home three years ago on April Fools Day, and I'm so glad I wasn't a fool and thought everything ended with Muffin. I believe God saw my grief and Babette's grief, and brought us together."

For some people, like Mary Lou of New Jersey, the "right time" to get a new pet may even be *before* the old pet dies. "The loss of our 18-year-old Standard Poodle was made less traumatic through the advice of a wonderful veterinarian," she wrote. "At first, we were not receptive to his kindly words of wisdom, for how can one respond to 'Do yourself and your dog a favor: Get a puppy now.'?

"Our Poodle was 10 years old at the time. Admittedly, she had grown too heavy and too lazy as a result of our overindulgence. The vet was aware of our extreme emotional attachment to her, and told us, 'Your dog needs a puppy to motivate her back to physical activity, and you need a puppy to absorb part of the love you devote to your 10-year-old.'

"We did not plan to take this advice, but a few months later a 4-month-old Standard Poodle was in need of a loving home, so we adopted her. Over the next eight years, the change in the 'old' dog was miraculous. And when she died, we had an 8-year-old in which to bury our tearful faces and find consolation. The loss of one was traumatic, but the presence of another devoted companion made it all bearable.

"Of course, our initial reaction was 'No more dogs after this one, it's just too much when they're gone.' But, three years ago a 12-week-old Doberman found her way into our home, so again, accidentally, we are abiding by the old vet's advice. History is repeating itself: The younger dog keeps the older dog active, and we spread our love between the two, knowing that when that frightful day comes again, the Doberman will help absorb part of the grief."

Clearly, only you can answer the question, "When is the right time for a new pet?" Andrea Z. of California wrote, "It depends on the individual when the time is right. You need to really be in touch with your feelings and realize the responsibility before obtaining a new pet. You must realize that a new pet will not be like the departed one. You must be patient and realize you are taking in a new personality and that it is not merely to take the place of the departed pet, for this can lead to problems. If you are unsure about obtaining a new pet, it's best to wait until you have sorted out your feelings, gotten over your grief, and have things in the proper perspective."

The answer will depend on your situation and how your grief is affecting you. If you are most affected by loneliness, a new pet right away may be the answer, but if you are suffering from anger and denial, this can spill over onto the newcomer and cause problems. You may wish to prepare yourself for your loss in advance, as many pet owners do, by always having more than one pet at a time, so that you are never without a loving companion. But the decision is a crucial one, and involves more than your own emotions: Too many pets are at animal shelters because they were adopted too soon and rejected by owners who were not emotionally ready to handle them.

Not a Replacement

Once you have made the decision to adopt a new pet, you need to be wary of a new problem: hoping that the new pet will be the image of the old. This is particularly likely to happen if you have adopted the new pet too soon, before you have had a chance to accept your loss. What you may be wanting at this time is not a new relationship, but a resurrection of the old one.

"One thing I would like to tell others who have lost a beloved pet," wrote Joyce, who found such happiness in Babette, "is that when you purchase another animal, remember that there will be a period of time when you will compare your new pet to the one that passed away. You will remember all the cute little tricks and things that your other pal did, and think that the new family member is not quite as good. Don't judge yourself for these feelings, because they're natural, and don't judge your new pet, because in a short time it will do things that make you love it just as much."

"After Cammie died, we dashed about madly to find 'another dog just like him,' " wrote Celia P. of New York. "The result is that we now have a sweet little girl who looks like a small Cam, but she's a nervous wreck. It was months before we stopped expecting her to be Cam and let her be herself. If you plan on another pet that looks like the last one, I think you should wait awhile, or else make up your mind to a constant battle with your emotions. That tiny replica is a little person in its own right, not your lost pet's reincarnation."

This reaction seems to a certain degree to be inevitable. Even if you have been without a pet for quite some time, bringing a new pet into the house is bound to remind you of your life with your old friend. You will see your new pet sleeping in the same place your old pet loved, or playing in the same yard, or eating from the same bowl, and it is easy and tempting to make comparisons. If you have not had many pets, and so have not experienced the wide range of personalities pets have, you may unconsciously anticipate that all pet/owner relationships will be the same, and that you will be able to simply pick up with the new animal where you left off with the old.

Pet owners recommend that, to avoid this reaction, you select a pet that is somehow different from the last. If you prefer a certain breed, select the opposite sex, for example. "Something about your new friend should be different from the old one," wrote Barbara T. of New Jersey. "Breed, size, color, sex, something! A 'duplicate' pet may not live up to the original in behavior, appearance or intelligence, but if the pet isn't a duplicate in looks, behavioral differences can be endearing rather than distracting."

Kathy D. of Oklahoma has some very specific suggestions on reestablishing a relationship with a pet. She advises that you look at more than just appearances, but examine your lifestyle and needs before making the decision.

"If you have lost a pet due to a contagious disease or because you were not equipped to care for it, getting another like it might only set you up for disaster," she points out. "In the case of disease, consult your veterinarian about the safety of the new pet. In some cases a well-immunized adult animal or an animal of a different species is the best choice, or a thorough disinfecting of your premises or a waiting period may be necessary. If an outdoor cat died of wounds received in a fight, or a dog was hit by a car while running loose, or some similar event occurred, some thought and preparation needs to be made or you may just set up another pet (and yourself) for the same tragedy.

"Give careful thought to a new pet. If your evaluation of your needs and what you have to offer makes you feel you should have one, it is an honor to the one who died, not a diminishment of your love for it.

"Use what you have learned from your previous pet(s) to select a new one, but be objective. You are selecting a companion for years to come. Look forward to your needs for those times, not backward to the past. Animals are as different from one another as are people, so don't expect a new pet of the same breed to be identical to the lost pet... If some similarities are particularly important to you, research the breed carefully and talk to several breeders. Seriously consider getting an adult animal that manifests the qualities you desire. It's unfair to expect a puppy or kitten to grow up into a certain kind of adult; there's no way to be sure, so think about it carefully if you know you wouldn't want it if it turns out 'wrong.'

"Getting a different type of pet may be best for you. Make sure the breed and individual pet you select is one whose needs you can meet, and that you are as sure as you can possibly be that the pet will be what you want. Whether the animal is a high-priced purebred or a shelter dog, have your vet check it, and be prepared to meet the animal's medical needs. If you can, get a healthy animal. If you are not sure of your ability to evaluate the animal's temperament, get help with this before adopting it. Temperament is not just 'good' or 'bad'—there are many variations of individual traits, and you need an animal whose temperament will please you as well as one you are able to handle. The *careful* selection of a new pet aids the healing process."

Though you may have made the distinction in your own mind between the old pet and the new, be alert to the reactions other family members are having as well. You want your new pet to be accepted and loved by the entire family, but other family members—especially children—may not have come to terms with their loss at the same rate that you have. "I strongly advise a family to wait until a child asks for another pet, rather than rushing to 'replace' a pet in an attempt to shorten everyone's grieving process," writes Muriel Franzblau of the Bide-A-Wee Home Association. "Before anyone else, the child must be ready for the new pet."

Carol of Kentucky didn't immediately realize how much her daughter Melanie was affected by the death of their dog Chadwick. "Not until we adopted Patrick did I start to see that she was still hurting deeply. After the newness of the puppy in the house wore off, I saw resentment starting to surface, and negative remarks. One day it suddenly hit me: She felt disloyal to Chadwick by allowing herself to love Patrick! When I finally realized what she was going through, I was able to talk to her about it, to explain that Chadwick had lived a long life; that we all loved him deeply, but if, in our lifetimes, we could allow ourselves to love only one dog, then most of our lives would be spent without any dog at all, because humans usually live longer than dogs do. After this, she was able to put it all in perspective, to thank God for the years He let us have Chadwick, and to realize it was time to allow herself to love another little dog."

Jenny B., a 14-year-old from Ohio, read my article "Coping With Sorrow" (*Dog Fancy*, September, 1986), and wrote me a moving and articulate letter about her feelings when the family dog, Brandy, died in June 1986. "I found it hard to show my emotions in front of my parents," she said. "But that night I cried myself to sleep, thinking it wasn't fair.

"In August we got a puppy. She is exactly the opposite of Brandy. Brandy was a Dalmatian. Although she was the runt of the litter, she was a big dog. The puppy (we haven't chosen a name yet) is a Poodle, black and very little. Just as one reader said in your article, I felt contempt for the puppy. It seems as though my parents praise everything she does, even if it isn't important. My dad had a nickname for Brandy and now he calls the puppy the same thing. I thought the name was special and only Brandy's. When he calls the puppy the nickname, I get upset and think he doesn't care about Brandy even though he is dead. I'm sure in time I will learn to like the puppy, but now I feel like I'm being disloyal to Brandy. I do play with her but some of the things she does reminds me of Brandy."

A letter like this couldn't go without answer. The following is a portion of my response:

"I don't think your father is intentionally uncaring; I'm sure he loved Brandy as much as you do. Perhaps his use of Brandy's nickname is an attempt to make himself feel better, to try and fill with the new dog the empty space Brandy left. He may, in a sense, be trying to 'replace' Brandy with the new dog—not in a bad sense, in trying to forget Brandy, but in the sense that he is hoping the new dog will become more like Brandy if he calls the dog by Brandy's nickname.

"If you can, you might wish to talk your feelings over with your father. If he hasn't read the article, show it to him. You both need to come to terms with the fact that the new dog is not Brandy, and cannot be compared to Brandy. You must learn to accept it on its own terms, learn what makes this dog unique and special in its own way, and let it earn its own nicknames. This takes time; grief doesn't heal overnight. You will never forget Brandy, but you won't be disrespectful of her memory by learning to love again. Don't expect it to happen instantly, and don't blame yourself for not being able to do it that fast—but give the dog a chance."

Many of the letters I wrote at *Dog Fancy* seemed to disappear into whatever void letters disappear into, never to be heard from again. But six months later, when I wrote back to Jenny to ask her permission to use her original letter in this book, I learned how the situation had turned out.

"We named our Poodle 'Ping'," she wrote. "The nickname problem has been resolved. My dad calls Ping a different nickname. I love Ping very much and realize she will never take the place of Brandy. Now my dad, after reading a copy of my letter and your response, realizes how I felt and why. He said he could understand how I felt and that he had many of the same feelings. My mom, dad and I concluded it is better to express your feelings in front of each other even though it is hard. That way no one has to second-guess how others feel."

Jenny's and Melanie's reactions are far from unusual, and are felt by pet owners of all ages. When you remember your departed pet, it is easy to focus on the good times and happy memories and forget the problems and hassles. The new pet hasn't had a chance to create happy memories of its own for you, so you may find yourself noticing only its flaws and shortcomings. Surely the departed pet didn't wet the rug nearly so often when it was young, or tear up the couch, or chew up your belongings, or make so much noise! What's wrong with this new pet, anyway? Why can't it be good like the last one? Caught between missing the good times with the old pet and the problems of adapting to a new pet in the household, you may find a lot of pain reawakening in your heart, even when you thought you had recovered from your grief—and it's easy to direct that pain at the newcomer.

As Joyce said earlier, it does you no good to judge yourself for these feelings; they are normal. Only time will enable you to view your new pet as an individual and get to know its own unique personality. But once you do, you will be infinitely rewarded. As R.M. of Illinois points out, "If you've got one ounce of love left after losing a dear one, share it with another, and watch that ounce overflow. Don't let an animal in need of just a drop of your love not get it, for they ask so little but give so much."

Chapter 6

The Most Painful Decision

IF THE DEATH OF A PET is the most painful event in a pet/owner relationship, then becoming the instrument of that death is understandably one of the most difficult things a pet owner ever has to do. Yet all too often we are faced with the day when we must make a life-or-death decision for a pet—and must, realistically, choose the latter.

Ironically, while this is a traumatic decision, it may also be the greatest act of love you can perform for your pet. It is the ultimate self-sacrifice; you are giving up a loving companion, a friend, an individual that has filled your life with joy and purpose, for its own sake. It is a decision that plunges you into the midst of all the agonizing emotions discussed in Chapter Two; their intensity will depend on the way you feel about your pet, as well as on your thoughts about life and death and about taking a life.

If you are caught up in that decision process now, or know that it lies ahead of you in the not-too-distant future, you may be wondering if this chapter will make euthanizing your pet any easier. I wish I could say yes, but I can't. Nothing can make that act easy, because no words I could write can balance out the years of love you've felt for your pet, or prevent the sorrow of anticipating or recalling its loss. What this chapter will do is show you when and why euthanasia is the right decision, and explore some of the options available to you when the decision is made.

Euthanasia and Guilt

Of all the emotions associated with euthanizing a pet, perhaps the strongest and most likely to occur—besides grief itself—is guilt. No matter how you rationalize the act, you are likely to return over and over to one central thought: You killed your pet. To some, that action is equivalent to murder.

Remember the feelings Susan G. described over the death of her dog? Guilt and anger were uppermost in her reactions. "I'm the one who took Junior there," she wrote. "I feel it's only right that I suffer now. I feel like I let Junior down and he trusted me." Susan's feelings are far from unusual.

Whenever something goes wrong in our lives, we have a tendency to ask what we did wrong to cause the problem, what we could have done differently to avert it, or what we did to deserve it. The answer, more often than not, is nothing, nothing and nothing. But somehow—whether due to the nature of the culture we live in, or a quirk of the human brain—it seems easier to assume personal responsibility, however farfetched, for unpleasant events in our lives than to write them off to fate or circumstances beyond our control.

When the event involves an action that we *can* point to, something definite that we did—regardless of the necessity of the action or the motive behind it—we have something to fasten our guilt onto. In the case of euthanizing a pet, you, the pet owner, must walk into a veterinarian's office or animal shelter and say, in whatever euphemistic terms you prefer, "Kill my pet." The vet may wield the needle, but you make the decision; in effect, you make the contract with the hit man. You are the person responsible for the pet's death. As Sue K. of Nebraska wrote, "I had to make the decision whether to let my friend live an uncomfortable life or to be his executioner."

To some, that action may truly feel like murder. To a pet owner like Susan, saying "kill my pet" is virtually equivalent to saying "kill my child." The less you regard your pet as an "animal" and the more you think of it as a "family member," the more you elevate your pet to human status, and the more euthanasia is equated with murder in your mind.

As if this weren't enough to arouse a strong guilt reaction, you may find a second factor adding to your misery: relief. Whenever a family member who has been suffering a long, difficult illness dies—especially if that illness has resulted in a significant loss of mental and/or physical function—it is normal and typical for the surviving family members to feel relief over the death. Survivors, especially the primary care-taker for the sick person, are glad for two things: that the person is no longer suffering and miserable, and that the bur-den of watching and coping with that person's suffering and needs has been lifted.

It is equally natural to feel relief when your pet is no longer in pain from its illness, or unable to function, enjoy life, or even enjoy contact with you and other family members. If your cat is a victim of kidney failure and is unable to control its bladder functions while clearly being in pain, or if your dog is so crippled by hip dysplasia that it can barely rise from the floor, you hurt to watch the suffering of the animal you love, and you are relieved when that suffering ends. At the same time, you may be relieved for your own sake: You will no longer have to medicate your pet, or hand-feed it, or clean up after it, or carry it from place to place.

But as you recognize this natural sense of relief, you may feel an extra load of guilt. "How can I even think that?" you may ask yourself in shocked horror. "I loved my pet; how could I have felt that taking care of it was too much trouble? I should have been less selfish, more caring; obviously I killed my pet for my own convenience, and I'm a terrible person." No chore, you think afterwards, should have seemed too difficult if it was for the benefit of your pet—you'd gladly do it all again, and more, if you could only have that beloved friend alive again. What an awful person you are for, in a sense, feeling glad that your pet is dead!

The very fact that you have these feelings—both the relief and the guilt—indicate that you are not a horrible person, but a normal one. The death of your pet has evoked strong emotional reactions in you, which are themselves indications of how much you loved and cared for your pet, and that you wanted the best for it. If you didn't love your pet or care what happened to it, its death would cause you little pain, and you wouldn't be coping with the trauma of bereavement now.

Reason and emotion have little in common; it's virtually impossible to rationalize away a strong emotion. However, it may help you to understand that coping with the needs of a sick or injured pet can be extremely stressful and wearing, and can even arouse resentment in you and the wish that your pet would die and free you of this tremendous burden. Few of us are able to put our own feelings and needs aside to the extent that we can be so self-sacrificing as to devote 100 percent of our efforts to the needs of another, with never a twinge of resentment or the wish that things weren't so difficult. Few mortals have achieved this level of saintliness, so try not to be too hard on yourself for not being one of them.

Both relief and guilt are normal reactions; do not condemn yourself for feeling either of them. However, keep in mind that relief is a *positive* reaction—however tragic your pet's death, you are aware at some level that things are now better both for your pet and for you. Guilt is a *negative* reaction that can cause you to view yourself and your actions in an increasingly bleak light if you allow yourself to dwell on it; in addition, guilt tells you that relief is a bad thing and that you shouldn't be feeling it. Again, though it is difficult to "reason" with emotions, it may help you to focus on the reality of the circumstances of your pet's death and of pet ownership in general, rather than letting guilt distort your view of the facts.

Many pet owners believe that prolonging a pet's suffering by avoiding euthanasia is the truly selfish action. These pet owners acknowledge that they will feel tremendous pain and loss when the pet is dead, but that what matters is the need of the pet, not the owner. They ask, "Is it right for me to force my pet to suffer just so that I won't have to?" To understand this perspective, let's take a closer look at the responsibilities pet ownership involves.

A wild animal or even a stray cat or dog has a sort of contract with nature. From its natural surroundings (even if those surroundings are alleys and vacant lots), the animal will find food, some sort of shelter from the elements, and social contact with its own kind. But when the animal becomes too sick, too badly injured or simply too old to hunt and function, nature takes over the other half of the contract. If the animal is not strong enough to recover, it will die—perhaps quickly at the claws of a predator or in a street accident, perhaps slowly through starvation and illness. In either case, death is virtually inevitable.

By removing animals from nature, we've taken on the duties of providing food and shelter and social contact—but we tend to shun the second half of the pact. Thanks to modern veterinary medicine, we are able to help our pets survive many types of illnesses and accidents that would, in nature, prove fatal. But eventually any pet reaches the point where it is too old, too sick or too badly injured to continue. Sometimes we can still prolong that pet's life, but only by prolonging its pain.

Sometimes we hope and pray that nature will step in and make the final decision for us—but all too often, that doesn't happen. Your pet can't make the choice for itself, and even if it could, it could not implement it. Your pet can't go to the veterinarian without you. The time has come to fulfill the second half of your contract—what some pet owners view as payment for the good times.

Knowing When It's Time

How do you know when the time has come to make the decision to euthanize your pet? Pet owners who have been through it offer a simple answer: when your pet can no longer live with dignity and without pain. Even then it's not an easy decision, and can be one that you tend to postpone. Maybe things will get better. Maybe a miracle will occur. Maybe one more treatment, one more surgery, or a different medication will make a difference. Maybe the pet will die in its sleep and take away the need for the painful decision.

"I prayed that he would just die during the night and I wouldn't have to make the decision I knew was inevitable," wrote Sue K. "But morning came and Tits was still alive. I knew that death would be kinder for him but it seemed that I just wouldn't be able to bear it without him."

"The hardest decision I had to make was whether to let my terrier live for my selfish needs, or put him out of his misery," wrote Gwen V. of New York. "It took me two days. I'd advise anyone whose dog has a hopeless illness to consider putting it 'down.' You are not doing your dog any favors by putting it through endless tests and surgeries to eke out a few precious months more of life together. Let go *before* the dog has suffered unbearably."

Gwen's message is clear and unmistakable: The only thing that matters in this decision is what is best for the pet, not what will be the most comforting or least painful for the owner. As you have so many times during the life of your pet, you must put the needs of the pet over your own emotions.

Cheryl T. of Alabama knows exactly what you're going through. "When my friend walked the floor all night gasping for breath because he could no longer breathe while lying down, I knew I had a decision to make," she wrote. "It was the most difficult decision I have ever made, and even though I knew it was right, I still felt like a traitor to Fred. I called the vet and told him I would bring Fred in on Saturday. The rest of the week I prayed he would pass away in his sleep, but Saturday came all too soon. When the vet examined him, he couldn't understand what was keeping the little dog alive, because even his kidneys had shut down."

"I can only tell you that March 14 was one of the saddest days of my life," wrote Mary P. of Louisiana. "I can only compare it to the deaths of my father and mother. That was the day I knew I had to have my Toy Poodle, Trina, put to sleep. She had breast cancer and had suffered terribly the night before. I finally admitted to myself that I was being selfish and just didn't want to let go, but it was best for her. I had hoped God would take her quickly and not force me to have to make that decision, but He didn't."

These three dogs were victims of combined factors: old age and incurable, terminal illnesses. In all three cases, the dogs were very close to death already, and while further medical care might have provided a few more days of life, these would have been painful days that would only cause the pet more suffering before the inevitable end.

That doesn't mean, however, that one must consider euthanasia at the first hint of illness. A pet may have a terminal illness and still have several good years ahead, if the owner is willing to invest the time, money and care needed to make those years pleasant and comfortable. If you have such a pet, you know that its time is limited, and you should be preparing yourself for the final decision even as you strive to make your pet's life full and happy. That's what Rose-Marie of Massachusetts did for her Poodle, Tammy.

Tammy began suffering from cancer at the age of 7. "She has been through three months of chemotherapy, cryosurgery, and finally, as a last-ditch effort, surgery to remove the tumor," wrote Rose-Marie. "The results were not encouraging because the vets found considerable bone erosion. As the vet put it, all we could do was wait and pray for a miracle to keep this cancer on hold."

Clearly Tammy couldn't survive her cancer long, so why had Rose-Marie chosen to prolong her life?

"People keep saying, 'Why do you bother spending so much money on a dog? Just put her to sleep!' " said Rose-Marie. "These people have never had as loyal a friend as Tammy. Tammy has many friends who are praying for her, too!" Her answer to these remarks: "We don't feel that she is suffering yet, so we're just going to love her for as long as we can. She continues to love everyone and tries her hardest to keep playing and enjoying life." Veterinary visits were turned into treats, complete with biscuits and extra loving from everyone involved. But Rose-Marie wasn't avoiding the decision; she knew it would have to be made sooner or later.

"I know that if and when this cancer starts to spread again, I will once again be faced with a painful decision," she wrote. "I have already promised that I will not let her suffer the way I have seen people suffer from cancer. When Tammy stops carrying around her ball and stops watching her friends 'the kitties' from the window and her voracious appetite disappears, I will know that she is telling me that she has lost her battle with cancer. But until then I will spend as much time and money as necessary to keep her well."

Several months after writing those words, Rose-Marie wrote again to say that Tammy had finally lost the battle, and that the promise had been kept.

Being There

Once you have made the decision to have your pet

euthanized, the next question is whether or not you should stay with the pet while the deed is done. That's a decision only you can make, based on whether or not you believe you can cope with the experience. Staying with your pet while it is put to sleep is not an easy thing to do. Examine what your decision will mean to you, what it might mean to your pet, whether your reactions will make the process more difficult for your pet, and how the action will affect you later.

"It may sound strange, but it helped me to help my dog die," wrote Linda C. of Texas, one of many pet owners who chose to stay with their pets to the end. "Jasper was terminally ill with cancer and had to be put to sleep. Now I take solace in having been with him during the last minutes of his life. Knowing that in his last moment he was comforted by the sound of my voice, the warmth of my touch and the love in my heart has helped me cope with his death.

"Though this course was right for me," Linda went on to say, "I would not recommend it to everyone. It took a tremendous amount of control to keep from going to pieces. I had promised Jasper that I would not let him suffer in any way, and that included the emotional suffering that would have been brought on by watching me break down. It was no easy task to maintain my composure.

"Death came gently to Jasper. There was no emotional pain, no panic that he might have experienced had I been absent. In the end, he went to sleep quietly in my arms. That gentle death was my parting gift to him—the culmination of my love for a cherished friend and companion."

"When it becomes necessary for my pets to be euthanized, I hold them as the injection is administered," wrote Pat H. of Pennsylvania. "I tell them how wonderful they are and how much they have meant to me. The last touch they feel is mine; the last voice they hear is mine. Believe me, this is not easy! When it's over, I'm a sobbing, quivering wreck! But I feel that I owe it to them—it's the last act of love I can give them to thank them for all they have given me."

"I felt I was closer than I had ever been with him and that I was able to say good-bye," agreed Donna D. of Maine.

But not everyone is able to face this emotionally devastating experience. Though the pet owners quoted above stayed for the sake of their pets, they would not have done so if they had felt their emotional reactions would have been upsetting to the pets. Other pet owners decided to stay away.

"I thought I could be strong and stay until the very end," wrote a California pet owner, "but my husband asked me to leave after the first injection. I'm glad I did."

"I couldn't take her to the vet," wrote Mary P. of Louisiana. "I knew I would fall apart completely. But I wanted her to be held in the last moments of her life by someone who loved her. My son, age 20, and daughter, 21, took her and held her. This was very difficult for them; Trina would have been 16 years old that May, and she was the first dog they had ever had."

Several pet owners regretted not being with their pets during the final moments. Some felt that they had missed out on an important step in finalizing and accepting the pet's death, on saying good-bye. Others were left with lingering doubts about what had actually happened: Had the pet suffered? Was the euthanasia actually carried out? What happened to the body? One pet owner even feared that her pet had not been euthanized, but might have been sold to a research laboratory. Clearly, staying with your pet through euthanasia is a sure way of laying your own fears to rest.

"I feel that if I had stayed with her, it would have made it easier for both of us," wrote Vivian R. of New Hampshire, whose wounded dog died at the veterinarian's office. "The vet told us that Pippy did not suffer because she was in shock, and that she would not have recognized me, but to this day I wish I had stayed with her."

Susan, who felt such guilt over the death of her St. Bernard, also felt guilt over not being there when her dog was euthanized. "The vet called and said he wanted to put Junior to sleep because he was suffering. He said I shouldn't come down while he did this. My husband and I were very upset and we did what he said. I'll regret this for the rest of my life." Later, another person told Susan that she should have been there; this only made Susan feel worse. "I was so attached to him that I still worry if he's suffering now, even though he's gone," she wrote.

From the moment you realize that euthanasia will be necessary, whether it is within the hour or months away, you will probably start wondering whether or not you should be present. It is not an easy decision. You may be torn between the pain you know you will experience by witnessing the death of your pet—and, in a sense, participating in it—and what you feel you owe to your pet. Though the final decision will be up to you, you should take some time to discuss the question with your veterinarian, or whoever will euthanize the pet. Find out what the facility's attitude is toward remaining with the pet; some clinics don't encourage owners to remain, as they aren't set up to handle the needs and reactions of a distraught and grieving owner. If you're sure you want to be present, ask your veterinarian for a referral to another clinic.

Keep in mind, too, that no caring veterinarian expects you to be a pillar of strength. Veterinarians know how much pets mean to their owners, and expect an emotional reaction. There is no reason to feel embarrassed over shedding tears in front of your veterinarian; in fact, if the veterinarian has known your pet for some time, or become close to it, don't be surprised if he or she joins you! "Owners may not realize it," says veterinary technician Katie K. of Florida, "but the staff (at least at our facility) feels a definite loss, too, when a patient dies or is put to sleep."

Whether you stay for the actual euthanasia or not, many pet owners agree that you should insist upon seeing the animal's body afterwards. "It is important to see and touch the deceased animal," says Rosemary S. of California. "This serves as confirmation that the animal is dead and did not appear to suffer, and it becomes more final in your mind. If someone takes the animal away before you can see it, you may always wonder if the animal was stolen, ran away, or may reappear one day. Also, you won't be so apt to be 'looking' for the missing animal. Finality is important. Once you accept that, you can go on to the future."

Easing the Passage

When you think of euthanasia, you may envision yourself putting the pet in the car, driving to the veterinary clinic or to a humane society, taking it into the facility and handing it over to a vet or a technician, and having it done. Some pet owners, however, believe this puts unnecessary stress on the pet (what pet likes to go to the clinic at the best of times?), and have worked out other ways to handle the process.

"In life our dog deserved and received no less than the best, and dying is a part of living," wrote Michaelene S. of Michigan. "Having your animal companion 'put to sleep' in your arms is, in my opinion, the method of choice. I realize that there are circumstances when this isn't possible, but I don't feel that putting your animal in a car, placing it on a metal table and walking away is a fitting memorial to someone who gave nothing but devotion and love.

"We made arrangements for our veterinarian to come to our house on a Friday afternoon. I called my girlfriend so she would be here to care for our German Shepherd, Tony. I bought a bottle of wine and selected a suitable container for Chuck's ashes. This was all done early in the week and I had several days not only to prepare myself emotionally for the 'letting go,' but to spend some real quality time with one of the most loving and best friends I'll ever have. That Friday my husband came home from work early and we spent the morning with Chuck, showing him birds, squirrels and chipmunks in our yard, and reaffirming to each other that this was the best and most humane act we could do for someone who never gave us anything but his very best.

"When the doctor arrived he confirmed what we had observed over the past few days. Chuck was beginning to suffer and there was no hope for a recovery or even to make him more comfortable with more medication. His lungs were beginning to fill with fluid and every breath was a supreme effort for him. My friend took the German Shepherd with her for the day, and we took my darling boy into our living room. As he was sitting on my husband's lap with me cuddling him and telling him what a good boy he was, he was peacefully put to sleep."

"Our dog, Ivan, was always afraid of the veterinary clinic," wrote Mary Z. of California. "I just couldn't stand the thought of him going out of this world in a state of panic. Because he would rather be in my van than anyplace else on earth—he loved that van and traveling—I made arrangements with our vet to come out to the van as soon as we got there. Ivan left the world in my van, in my arms. I've always had the feeling that for once I did the right thing at the right time."

One pet owner suggests that, even if the pet is sick and has been in the hospital, it should be brought home "for at least one night, even if it's the last night, just so the end isn't spent in the strange and fearful surroundings of the veterinary hospital." This pet owner then has a friend drive her to the clinic, while she sits in the back seat and talks soothingly to the dog. Like Mary, she asks that the veterinarian come out to the car to give the final injection.

Barbara H. of Maryland suggests that you "ask your veterinarian for a strong sedative that can be given to the animal at home in a favorite food. Hold the animal until it is deeply asleep, then carry it to your vet for the last time. It is a minor thing, but can make it much easier on all concerned. The pet is already asleep, so the vet and the family don't have to cope with a terrified animal. This is what we did with our old dog, and my husband stayed with him until he died—we felt we owed him that much. His passing was peaceful and gentle, and our sorrow was somewhat eased by that fact."

"The vet agreed that I could give Titsie the preliminary medication at home so that he'd be asleep when he made his last trip across town to the clinic," wrote Sue K. "He had always hated and feared riding in the car. That was how I wanted it for him—no fear and going to sleep with me near— but it made me feel even more like an executioner. I didn't think I could actually give the injection. But, with the help of the presence of a friend, I was able to give the shot and Titsie drifted off to sleep in my arms calmly and without fear."

If such a course of action seems right for you, discuss with your veterinarian whether or not he or she is willing to go along with your plan. If you can't make such arrangements with your regular vet, ask if he can recommend another veterinarian who could perform this service; in some areas there are "mobile" veterinarians who will come to your home.

If you have a little time, it can help you to spend a few days getting yourself used to the idea of parting with your pet, a period of saying good-bye. You might wish to spend extra time with the pet, perhaps taking it to visit old haunts that it loved, or fixing it special meals of its favorite foods—

even foods that haven't been on its diet previously due to its health. You may find, in some uncanny way, that your pet somehow senses what is happening and seems to make a special effort to say good-bye to you, as well. This happened to me when my parents decided to euthanize our aged and sick Norwegian Elkhound. The night before her last trip to the vet, she came around to each family member and sat down for several minutes for a long, solemn love session—something she had never done before. I was convinced that she knew her time had come, and was saying good-bye in her way to her loved ones.

Chapter 7

Choosing a Final Resting Place

WHEN YOUR PET DIES, you have one decision still to make: what to do with its remains. You have several choices, and this chapter will discuss the most common methods of disposal. These are: leaving the body with a veterinarian or shelter, home burial, cemetery burial, cremation, and preservation. Each option has advantages and disadvantages.

Your choice is likely to be influenced by a number of factors, including the options available to you in your area, cost, your emotional reactions to the pet's death, and your personal and/or religious values and beliefs. It's difficult to take these factors into careful consideration when you are in the midst of coping with the trauma of your loss; this is not an easy time to sit down and logically and dispassionately evaluate costs and options. In addition, once your pet has died, you are faced with an immediate need to make a decision, which robs you of the time required to make an informed, well-thought-out choice. This is liable to place more stress and anguish upon your shoulders when you need it the least.

It is far better to make this decision well in advance of the death of your pet. To some, such advance planning may seem painful or downright ghoulish; many people go through life with the attitude that if they don't think about death or ac-knowledge mortality—their own or their pets'—they can some-how miraculously avoid the inevitable. Planning for your pet's disposal while it is still alive and healthy is rather like writ-ing a will: You'd rather not think about it, and it often gets put off until it's too late. Instead of thinking of this process as accepting the inevitability of your pet's death, think of it as providing yourself with peace of mind. When the time comes to follow up on your plans, you'll be very glad you made them when you did.

To plan for the disposal of your pet's remains, you'll need to investigate the options available in your area. For example, if you would like to have your pet buried in a cemetery, you'll need to determine if one exists near you, or decide whether it is worth traveling a great distance to find one.

As you make your plans, you may want to think not only of what your situation is now, but what it is likely to be when your pet dies. Will your financial situation be better or worse? Will you be able to afford the method of disposal of your choice? Will you still be living in the same area? Will you live in any area for a long time, or do you expect to move around a great deal? Do you want to make the same choice for all your pets, both those you presently own and those you will own in the future—or do you want to make special arrangements for one particular pet? You need to determine the most appropriate choice based on your estimated needs and resources at the time of your pet's death.

Veterinary or Shelter Disposal

When a pet dies or is euthanized at a veterinary clinic, many owners who haven't made advance plans are completely unprepared to deal with the body. Not knowing what else to do, they often take the easiest course of action: They let the veterinarian handle everything. Any veterinarian will dispose of your pet's body if you ask, or if you don't specify that you want to make other arrangements. In the midst of your grief and shock, this may seem the least painful option, and in some cases it is the best.

In other cases, however, especially in busy clinics or in clinics that don't take the emotional needs of an owner into account, this may be a choice your veterinarian pressures you into making, directly or indirectly. The veterinarian may not be aware of the other options available in the area, and thus have no answer to your question, "What else can I do?" Since a veterinarian's first priority is the care and treatment of living animals, he may simply not have the time or facilities to sit down and discuss disposal options with a distraught owner who may be in no condition to make a rational decision in the first place. That's why it is important for you to be informed about the choices you can make in advance, rather than relying on someone else to help you through this decision at the last minute.

In most cases, when you leave your pet's body with a veterinary clinic, the clinic will arrange for its cremation. Some clinics turn the remains over to a county facility such as an animal shelter to handle cremation.

The same goes for pets left at shelters or humane societies. Since these facilities often offer euthanasia services, they, too, are frequently left with the pets' remains. Some shelters even have disposal bins on their property in which pet owners, or anyone who has reason to dispose of a dead animal, can leave the remains. These remains are often cremated along with those of the many unwanted pets that the society is forced to euthanize during its normal operations.

There is another, less pretty possibility when you leave your pet at either type of facility, however. Instead of cremating your pet, the facility may send its body to a rendering service. Such a service boils down animal remains for fat and other by-products, which are used in a variety of types of products—including, according to one California pet owner who investigated this practice, "wax, makeup, fertilizer, soap, chicken feed and dog food." I'm not going to open up a discussion of the ethics or desirability of this practice here, but you should be aware that this possibility exists, and if it disturbs you, it is one more excellent reason to make your choices *before* you are forced to do so in haste. Ask your veterinarian or shelter employee exactly what will happen to your pet's remains at that facility.

A few veterinarians, usually in rural areas, offer funeral services of their own if they have property on which they can bury pets. "A kind-hearted rancher donated a section of land to our vet for pet burials, and that's where our dogs' physical remains rest," wrote Minta S. of Texas. "They remain in our minds and hearts." Generally, such burials are in the form of unidentified "country" graves, which may contain several animals, rather than in the form of a formal pet cemetery. However, a few veterinarians also operate pet cemeteries; indeed, this country's oldest pet cemetery, the Hartsdale Canine Cemetery in New York, began as a service provided by a caring country vet who began to inter pets in his apple orchard in the late 19th century.

One factor that often influences the decision to leave a pet's body at the clinic or shelter is cost. Often, there is no additional charge for disposal if a pet dies at a clinic. Some clinics do charge extra, but this amount is often far less than you would have to pay elsewhere for more formal handling of the pet's remains. Some clinics will also handle remains of pets that have died at home and are brought to the clinic, for which there is usually a small fee. It's a good idea to ask your veterinarian in advance about the fees charged for disposal.

There is no charge for leaving a pet in a disposal bin at an animal shelter, but shelters and animal control services may charge a small pickup fee if called to remove an animal from your premises. In some areas, it is illegal to place an animal's remains out for normal trash pickup, though this applies primarily to large animals, not small birds or rodents. In some areas you can call your local sanitation department for a special pickup at no cost, but in others you may be charged a fee.

If your pet's death catches you unawares, without advance plans, it's a good idea to ask your veterinarian if he can allow you a grace period in which to make up your mind. Some clinics, if they have the space and resources, will freeze your pet's body and hold it for a few days, until you are better able to decide whether or not you want to reclaim it and handle its disposal yourself. Again, it's a good idea to find out if your veterinarian will offer you this choice before you need it.

Thus the advantages of leaving a pet at a veterinary clinic are cost and convenience. The veterinarian makes all the arrangements, and if there is a charge, it will generally be less than you would pay for a cemetery burial or cremation.

Carol H. of Delaware noted an additional advantage in her case: "We hoped our dog would, even in her death, help someone understand the mystery of bloat. When you lose a pet, remember before you pay the crematorium or pet cemetery that research is very important. Self-indulgence is useless when you could just as easily save a pet who is as precious to someone else as yours was to you [by donating your pet's body to veterinary research]."

On the other hand, this option leaves you little say in how your pet's remains are handled, which can be disturbing to some pet owners, like Nancy P. of Washington. "My very deep and lasting regret is that I left my dog there and never got him back," wrote Nancy. "I wish very much I had at least gotten his ashes back to bury at home. I was too upset at the time to think straight and to realize I wouldn't have him anymore. Now, I don't even have a part of him here, at home, where he should have been put to rest. I will not make the same mistake with my other dogs when the time comes."

Veterinary or shelter disposal is a good option for someone who believes that the important part of a pet is its soul or spirit, that intangible essence of personality that leaves the body at death, rather than its physical remains. Many people believe that a body is just a shell, empty and meaningless once the spirit has left it, and that the departed pet has no interest in what happens to that shell. Such pet owners argue that what is important is how you cared for your pet during its life, and believe that your energies and resources after its death should be devoted to the love and care of future pets.

Others, however, view a pet's body more as a shrine than as a shell, deserving of a resting place that symbolizes the honor and love the pet received during its lifetime. Some feel that their pets are near as long as their remains are near. I mentioned memorials in Chapter Three as a good coping strategy, and a pet's grave can be the ultimate memorial. The choice is highly personal, and should be made with a clear mind and with your own values and beliefs taken into consideration;

otherwise you may find yourself rushed into a decision you will later regret.

Home Burial

One of the most popular methods of disposing of a pet's remains is burial at home. Pet owners who wrote about home burial described it as the natural extension of one's love for a pet, the final way of keeping the pet close to its loved ones, and a warm family ritual.

One advantage of home burial is that it is virtually cost-free, especially if you make your pet's casket yourself. Another is that it keeps your beloved pet close by, always available for a visit or a reminiscence. Tending the grave is up to you, and costs you nothing more than your time; you can decorate it with flowers from your own garden, or choose a place that nature will decorate in its own way.

Some pet owners feel that home burial is what their pets would have preferred. "I believe that pets should be put to rest somewhere near their original homes, where they felt secure and loved during their lifetimes," wrote Lee Ann of Georgia. "I always bury my pets in their own backyard or in a patch of woods nearby, where their spirits can look out over the domain they occupied in life."

Cammie, a Pug owned by Celia P. of New York, loved flowers, so his ashes are buried in the backyard rose garden. "We chose the rose garden because Cam spent a lifetime of frustration over not being allowed to touch the roses. He smelled the flowers at will, but roses have thorns, and no Pug with its vulnerable eyes is allowed to pick roses. Peonies he brought in joyfully after every trip outside when they were blooming. Now, every time the flowers bloom, I can see him bouncing around out there. Yes, it brings a little pang. But it also makes me realize that you never really lose a beloved pet; the memories are a permanent treasure."

"My children like knowing he's there and say they don't want to move," wrote Jan R. of Tennessee. Often the act of the funeral itself can be a comforting family ritual, providing a means for family members to come together in their grief and acknowledge their loss. "I helped make the box and dig the hole," wrote Rhonda H. of Michigan. "It's sad to talk about it, but I'm glad I did it. It helped me cope with his death, and I know he was comfortable with his favorite blanket."

"Decide what funeral rites you desire while your pet is young," urged Melody M. of North Carolina. "We live in a rural area and have a pet cemetery on the farm. We make the coffin; as it is finally lowered and still open, we place flowers around our pet, as well as its toys and other possessions. We then place bricks on the coffin lid to prevent predators from vandalizing the grave."

"Whenever we lose a pet, we have a funeral for it," wrote Carol F. of Kentucky. "We live in the woods, where that is permissible. We bury the pet with a favorite toy and mark the grave, and occasionally pluck flowers to take to their little cemetery." Carol notes that "other pets are not permitted to take part in the funeral. We have never felt it was wise for them to know where a companion was buried, for fear they might dig the body up."

Holly T. of Arizona has no such fears. "In the past when I buried dogs in my backyard—illegal? Be damned!—my other dogs would gather around. They never dug up the remains, but they did 'visit' the gravesite, sitting quietly beside the little mounds. The closer the relationship, the longer the visitations lasted."

Holly's comment points out one of the primary disadvantages of home burial: In many areas, it is illegal. Most urban areas, concerned about sanitation, prohibit the burial of pets in yards within city limits. Even when home burial is permitted, usually in rural areas, you are liable to find rules about size limits on animals to be buried and about the depth of the grave. A grave should be deep enough that no smells can escape, and that predators cannot dig up the remains.

Most pet owners, however, simply perform their ceremonies carefully and quietly, without attracting the attention of the authorities. Pet owners with additional pets or with concerns about hygiene are likely to observe appropriate grave depths in any case, and pet owners who "break the rules" by burying pets at home are well aware that most cities don't have the manpower to check backyards for illegal burials. However, it is advisable, should you choose this route, to be discreet with ceremonies and grave markers, as your neighbors may not be thrilled by the presence of a miniature cemetery in your yard.

The size of your property will certainly influence the size of the animal you are willing to have buried there. Small birds can easily be buried in a yard of any size, and their remains do not last long; however, remains of an animal even the size of a cat require some careful thought. "The animal warden in our village advised me on the 'Q.T.' that if the neighbors did not complain, a small- to medium-size pet could be buried in our backyard," wrote Jean-Irene of Illinois. "However, Wolfe was 45 pounds, and I know it would not have been the best place for him, because we would constantly be seeing the grave and marker. It would be too heartbreaking."

Even if pet burial is legal on property you own, it isn't legal on property you do not own. If you rent a house in the city, you have no legal right to bury a pet on that property—nor, probably, would you want to, for renting implies impermanence. You wouldn't want the next tenant to acquire the grave of your pet along with the rest of the house, would you?

That brings up the second major disadvantage to home burial: mobility. "One of the hardest things I ever did was to move away and leave behind the cat I had buried in the backyard," wrote Christine A. of California. Today, people move considerably more often than in the past, especially single adults and young families. While your parents may have lived in the same location for 30 or 40 years, you may move many times in that same time-period. If you own property, you will probably sell it when you leave, and your pets' remains along with it. Some people solve that problem by digging up pets' remains and taking them along, but for most this is impractical, particularly if you have buried several pets. A better solution is to have your pets buried on rural property owned by a friend or relative—but again, many pet owners don't have that option available. Pet owners who know they will move frequently often opt for cremation, because ashes can be transported easily. Cremation is discussed later in this chapter.

Cemetery Burial

Those who can't or would prefer not to bury their pets at home, but still wish to see the animals' remains "decently interred," often choose burial at a pet cemetery. Pet cemeteries aren't available everywhere, and prices vary widely from one to the next; at some, plots may start at $50 to $65, while at others, a burial with lots of options such as perpetual care, casket, marker or monument and opening and closing costs can run well over $1,000.

However, many pet owners feel that a pet cemetery provides a sense of permanence and security that makes any cost worthwhile. Such owners see the formality and dignity of such a burial as a fitting tribute to a beloved friend, and enjoy the comfort of knowing that the pet is in serene surroundings and that the gravesite will be well cared for. They also enjoy being able to visit the grave at any time.

"We put all six of our dogs, over a time span of 32 years, in the lovely J.L. Bowling's Pet Cemetery in Teays Valley," wrote Evelyn S. of West Virginia. "Nearly 100 people are buried in the cemetery with their pets. It really helps to give your pets a final resting place that you can visit. It keeps your dogs 'alive' in your memory. Burying them in a lovely place with other pets (with perpetual care, too) is the last act of gratitude you can provide for a pet that has spent its life making you happy."

"For me the only answer was burial in a pet cemetery," said Patricia C. of Ohio. "Knowing the land is dedicated and never to be disturbed by construction or the like is what sold me on this idea. You can go out there any season, any day and reminisce. For 12 years now my brother and I have gone out and looked at our pets' graves; we put flowers on them, cut the weeds around them, and even wash the gravestones. Just knowing their remains are there is to know I gave my pets the best after death."

Eva D. of Arizona wrote that "pets are just like any other member of the family. Therefore, they deserve the same treatment upon their deaths that you would afford a human." Judi P. of Illinois agreed: "It helped me tremendously to know she was treated with the love and respect she deserved. I was glad she went in style, not just discarded like yesterday's trash. I am so glad I can visit her."

"I tend to think my little dog's spirit is happy and content with his canine friends in this lovely retreat, with its beautiful setting," wrote Shirley O. of California. Linda C. of Texas found that cemetery burial was important to her personally, as well as for the memory of her pet. "I didn't understand how important a gravesite is to the grieving process until Jasper died," she wrote. "I had an intense bond with Jasper and my need to love and care for him didn't cease just because he was no longer physically present. Caring for his grave allowed me to continue, indirectly, to care for Jasper and, in turn, gradually helped me to come to accept his death."

Most cemeteries maintain a rural image, even if they are in the heart of a city. Smooth lawns, graceful trees and pleasant shrubbery convey the image of a peaceful and serene final resting place. Amidst this serenity, many options are usually available. Depending on the cemetery, you may be able to purchase individual plots for each of your pets, or you may select a plot that will hold two to four pets, depending on their size. In some cemeteries, as Evelyn noted, it is even possible to be buried with or alongside your pets. In some cemeteries, an inexpensive "farm burial," which is a mass burial of pets in an unmarked grave, is still available, but this practice has fallen into disfavor and is being widely discontinued.

The type of plot you desire isn't your only choice. Do you want the grave tended by mortuary personnel, or do you want to take care of it yourself? Some cemeteries don't have the facilities to keep graves trimmed and neat; others offer a "perpetual care" package that will handle this for you for either a flat, one-time fee or an annual charge. You may also be able to purchase regular floral decoration of your pet's grave; Hartsdale Canine Cemetery, for example, provides seasonal flowers or greenery grown on the premises.

You may wish to purchase a casket, headstone, marker or other types of "accessories" at the mortuary, or you may wish to purchase those separately. You can obtain caskets of every imaginable material, marble stones with custom inscriptions, flat engraved markers, monuments and just about anything else you desire.

Along with a choice of products, you have some choice in ceremonies. You might wish to write your own eulogy, or have the mortuary select appropriate services. Check with the individual cemetery as to whether you can conduct the ceremony yourself (or arrange for a friend or minister to do so), or whether it must be conducted by cemetery personnel. Or, you can have your pet interred with no ceremony at all. In many cases, for a small fee you can arrange for your pet's funeral to be recorded on film or videotape.

Some cemeteries have arrangements with veterinary clinics for pickup. In this case, once you've made arrangements with the cemetery and reserved your plot, all you have to do when the time comes is instruct your veterinarian to contact the cemetery. Many cemeteries will also pick up a pet directly from your home, though there is usually a fee for this service. Many cities also have "pet taxi" or "pet limo" services, which are very convenient for people who have difficulty transporting their pets.

The primary disadvantage of a pet cemetery, obviously, is cost. The range of services available is extensive, but the more services and products you choose, the higher your bill will be. Some pet owners have decided against cemetery burial because they would prefer to spend the money on their living pets. Others realize that though they might be able to afford to bury one special pet in a cemetery, the cost of burying every beloved pet would be prohibitive. Mobility is another disadvantage: If you move away, you will leave your pet's remains behind and will no longer be able to visit them. However, you will have the peace of mind of knowing that you leave them in good hands.

There are occasional exceptions even to this assumption, however. In the past several years, a handful of cases have arisen in which pet cemeteries have been sold to developers. The pet cemetery formerly operated by the Los Angeles SPCA, containing such famous animals as Hopalong Cassidy's horse and the MGM lion, is an example. When the society wished to sell a part of the land that was not being used for burials to a developer, pet lovers rose up in arms over this decision, claiming that development would jeopardize the integrity of the cemetery. Ultimately, this group of pet owners, which named itself SOPHIE (Save Our Pets' History in Eternity) bought the cemetery and is now managing it. A similar case arose in 1986 in Maryland, provoking an equally emotional reaction; the cemetery also contained human burials.

Cases like these make some pet owners cautious about choosing a cemetery. "I suggest a certain amount of investigation to assure yourself that there is little danger of the cemetery land being sold or your pet being uprooted," advises Eva D. "Ask questions of the owners—do they own the land and what are their plans for the future of the pet cemetery, and any other questions that would help determine if the cemetery is a safe place to put your beloved pet. Make sure the cemetery is kept up and is safeguarded against vandalism." Make sure, also, that the grounds are restricted for use as a cemetery, so that they will never be used for another purpose.

Cremation

Cremation allows you to do whatever you wish with your pet's remains: You can bury the ashes, scatter them, or carry them with you wherever you go. Or, the pet's ashes can remain in a niche at a columbarium. If there are no pet crematoriums near you, you may be able to arrange for the individual cremation of your pet through your veterinarian or humane society.

"I had decided long in advance that Trina would be cremated, and her ashes will go with me wherever we live," wrote Mary P. of Louisiana. "I have friends who buried their dogs in the yard, sold their houses later, and seriously regretted leaving their beloved pets behind. Trina's ashes will be moving with me in a month, and I'm so glad I made that decision."

"I feel a great peace in knowing Chuck was cremated," wrote Michaelene S. of Michigan. "I managed to locate an urn with a picture of a Cocker Spaniel on it and had my veterinarian place his ashes in it for me. I have a grandfather clock in the living room, and the ashes are locked in the clock case along with the ashes of Cinnamon, who belonged to one of my friends. She didn't have a spot in her home that would make a suitable resting place, so she decided that both dogs should rest together in my home. I have delayed either spreading the ashes or burying them because once a week when the clock must be opened and wound, I find great peace in seeing the urns and knowing that my darling is safe and sound. He was such a good and precious friend that I cannot bear to part with his remains at this time."

Michaelene is one of many pet owners who have chosen to keep their pets ashes in their home. Sue K. keeps the ashes of her cat Titsiepritzel in a "beautiful aspen-wood box, intermingled with the petals of a red rose." Cathy W. of California keeps her Poodle's ashes in a golden urn, for which a friend made a plaque with the dog's name, dates and an inscription. Several pet owners have found ways to incorporate such urns—which come in a wide range of beautiful, decorative styles, sizes, shapes and materials—into memorial tributes to their pets. You can find listings of a number of companies that produce such products in the classified sections of the major pet magazines, such as *Dog Fancy, Cat Fancy, Dog World,* or *Purebred Dogs/AKC Gazette.*

Other pet owners, like Jacqueline R. of New York, are keeping their pets' ashes to be interred with their own. "I had my Hurky cremated and have his ashes here, as I will with them all," wrote Jacqueline. "When it's time for us all to be put to rest, we will all go to one place together." Shirley P., a bird owner living in Idaho, wrote that she hoped to have her ashes and those of her birds sent into orbit, having read about a company that offered this service for around $10,000. "Think of it," she wrote. "Your ashes will orbit the earth for about 60 million years before the orbit decays. Above all the turmoil and troubles of earth! Hopefully this will become more popular (and cheaper) as time goes by."

Many pet owners choose not to keep their pets' ashes, but to scatter them. "I had my dog cremated and let the ashes blow over the ocean that he loved to play in," wrote Donna D. of Maine. Maureen O. of California wrote: "I take the ashes up to the hills or river and scatter them myself. I wouldn't want to keep them, because I wouldn't want to get depressed and sit and cry over them. They should be out in the air and land where they originated, and free, not in a jar."

"When our beloved 12-year-old Cocker Spaniel, Sir Higgins, died, I kept thinking about how I wanted to take him to the ocean, but never did, using the excuse that it wouldn't be fair to Lady Tiffany, our 5-year-old Cocker, who couldn't go because of severe hip dysplasia," wrote counselor Maurine J. Sauters. "So, I told him after he died that he was still going to go, and when I picked up his ashes I took my wonderful, special boy to the beach. I sat on a log for over an hour talking to him about the birds, the surf, the boats, the people, the other dogs. Then we went home. The next day my husband, Lady Tiffany, and I took Higgins to our church, where our pastor prayed with us and then buried the ashes in the garden."

Cremation is not always cheap; the cost usually depends upon the size of the pet. However, it is readily available, and you will get the best price if you do your research and make your arrangements in advance. Cremation does increase your options on what to do with your pet; it even makes home burial an easier proposition.

Preservation

The least common and most controversial choice for handling your pet's remains is to preserve them. In the past, this meant taxidermy; now, however, the option of freeze-drying is available, and is a vast improvement over the older method. Advocates of freeze-drying say that this method leaves the pet much more life-like, and the preservation is longer-lasting, without chemicals. The method was developed for the preservation of museum specimens, and works well for birds as well as for dogs and cats.

When *Cat Fancy* ran an article several years ago that described freeze-drying and taxidermy as options for the "disposal" of a pet, the magazine received dozens of letters from shocked pet owners who thought this was a morbid, repulsive idea. One dog owner wrote that she received "a terrible reaction" from family and friends. Other pet owners, however, wrote that they approved of this possibility and described it as a way of keeping one's pet close at hand forever, in a more realistic manner than as a handful of ashes in an urn.

Many taxidermists now have the equipment to freeze-dry animals, particularly smaller pets. Like any other disposal option, this is a matter of personal choice and taste. If you choose preservation, however, you should be prepared for some lack of understanding from others. However, your choice should be based on what you feel is right for you and for your pet, not on the opinions of others.

Your selection of a "final resting place" for your pet will undoubtedly be a function of the unique combination of circumstances, values and desires that influence your life. You will need to decide whether your pet's memory, enhanced by photos or other types of tributes, is enough without the nearness of its physical remains, or whether those remains are also important to you. Your choice should also take into account whether you plan to live in the same place for most of your life, or whether you plan to move around a lot. Your financial condition will play a role in the decision, as will the resources available to you in your community.

Most importantly, though, the decision must be yours. It should not be forced upon you from outside, through the well-meaning opinions of friends or relatives. It should not be forced on you by a veterinarian who is anxious to get on to his next client. The best way to ensure that you are able to make your own decision, the best decision for your situation and your pet, is to give the matter thought before the situation arises. Gather information on your options ahead of time. If your choice is an expensive funeral and you don't know if you'll have the money when the time comes, make arrangements now to start paying for the funeral in small amounts. It's not easy to think about your pet's death and disposal while it is still young and active and bouncy—but it's even tougher when the sad event actually happens.

Chapter 8

The
Missing Pet

REVIOUS CHAPTERS have discussed ways to cope with a pet's death. But there is another kind of trauma that can be just as difficult to face, and even more difficult to resolve: the loss of a pet. If your pet escapes from its home or yard, or is stolen, or runs off while traveling with you, you are thrust abruptly into a frustrating, frightening and potentially devastating experience that may carry with it all the painful emotions associated with pet death.

Many pet owners say that losing a pet in this way is even worse than losing it to death, because of the uncertainty involved. When a pet disappears, it is lost to you, often permanently—but you do not have the assurance of knowing what happened to it. You do not have the chance to accept the finality of its death by viewing its body or handling its funeral arrangements. You have no chance to prepare for the loss, as you would with a pet that is old or ill. Nor do you know whether the pet is gone forever or will reappear, whether it is dead and at peace or suffering somewhere, whether it has been adopted into a good home or is wandering the streets as a stray. Few things are as difficult to cope with as uncertainty.

Added to this agony of uncertainty are all the classic elements of grief. When a pet disappears, you face much the same situation as if it had died: the disruption of your routines, the hole in your life, the conspicuous absence of the beloved animal in your daily interactions. The pet's disappearance will certainly trigger sorrow as you force yourself to contemplate the fact that your pet might be dead; it may also arouse all the other emotions described in Chapter Two, and then some. Guilt: "If only I hadn't left the gate open; it's all my fault he got loose!" Anger: "Why can't the animal control people do anything? How could you have been so careless? How could Fido have been so stupid as to run off?" Depression and despair: "There's nothing I can do. He'll never come home. He's out there suffering somewhere and I can't help him." Frustration: "No one cares! The shelters don't care! The police won't help! There's nothing I can *do!*" Denial: "He'll come back. He'll show up tonight... tomorrow... the next day. He's just out doing the town."

The hardest part of the situation is that, even though you are experiencing part of the bereavement process, there is no final moment at which you can say, "Now is the time to start grieving." When a pet dies, you know that an ending has been made, and your grieving process can begin at that ending. When a pet is missing, grief and hope constantly battle for supremacy; one day you may decide to admit that your pet is gone for good, but the next day you may feel a surge of hope that it will return, the phone will ring, someone will have seen it, it will show up on your doorstep. When the grieving process is constantly interrupted or put on hold, it can go on much longer and be much more difficult to resolve than it would be if the pet had died.

In addition, you may be reluctant to use some of the coping strategies recommended for dealing with the death of a pet. As long as you still have hope that the pet will return, you may not want to put away its toys or dishes. Creating a memorial such as a photo collage may be a more blatant statement that your pet is gone than you are ready to make just yet. You may postpone getting a new pet much longer than you would if the original pet had died, because what are you going to do with two pets if the first comes home again?

Some of the coping strategies *can* help, however. If you

have other pets, focus on them as much as possible, for they may be as concerned over their companion's absence as you are. Devote a portion of your energies to making sure that whatever caused the loss of the missing pet can't happen to the remaining animals. Talk to caring friends about your grief and confusion of feelings. Allow yourself to cry, to be angry, to feel your guilt and your pain and to express these emotions. If you have access to a bereavement counselor, find out if he is willing to help you with this kind of loss. If you can find consolation in your faith, remind yourself that God understands and cares in this time of pain.

Unlike the death of a pet, this kind of loss is not inevitable. Many pet owners never have to face it. But all too many do, and it is a possibility you should be prepared for. Nothing can guarantee that you *won't* experience such a loss, but there are steps you can take to make it less likely, and if it does happen, there are steps you should take immediately to greatly enhance your chances of regaining your pet. Prevention is the best medicine, as the saying goes; in addition, having a careful recovery plan in mind before you need it can make a tremendous difference.

Prevention

It is a sad fact that many pets disappear due to their owners' lack of awareness of potential hazards and escape routes. One problem about regarding a pet as a family member is that many people tend to consider their pets *too* human. While pets may display many human traits, they still have the instincts and urges of their species, and these can lead them into trouble. So when you look at your pet's environment, look at it from the animal's perspective as well as your own.

Dogs, for example, are generally excited by and attracted to other dogs. It is not uncommon for a dog to join up with a pack of strays that happens to wander through the neighborhood, and run off for a day of romping and exploring. By the time your dog thinks about returning home, it may be far away from familiar territory.

Cats, especially unneutered toms, tend to be roaming animals. Even a cat that usually spends its time close to home may discover a new attraction one day and change its schedule, which can drive a pet owner nuts! On the other hand, don't let an animal control officer dismiss your fears over the disappearance of a cat with an offhand "Oh, all cats like to wander; don't worry about it." The sudden disappearance of a cat that has never voluntarily stayed out overnight in the last five years is a genuine cause for concern.

Unaltered cats and dogs are driven by the mating urge. A male may travel great distances to follow up the airborne scent of a female in heat. A female in season may wander off with her beau, oblivious to anything but this newfound passion. Pets driven by the mating urge often seem to go suddenly deaf to human commands.

One of the best things you can do to guard against a runaway pet is to have your pets spayed and neutered at an early age. This action will not only reduce the risk of your pet running off in search of a mate, but will minimize its vulnerability to death from cancer of the reproductive organs, or from one of the many possible complications of pregnancy. Neutering a male cat while young may nip its wandering tendencies in the bud; however, if you wait until the cat is mature, neutering may not have much effect on habits that have already been formed. Spaying a female cat or dog before its first heat—and especially before a pregnancy—reduces the health risk of such surgery. In addition, your action not only protects your own pets but cuts down on the number of unwanted pets that must be euthanized every year due, in a large part, to pet owners who fail to take this simple precautionary step.

If you own a dog in an urban area, the most important thing you can do to safeguard it against loss or accident is to make sure it is confined in some way at all times. A dog that roams free in such an environment is marked for disaster. At any time it could fall victim to a traffic accident; malicious or accidental poisoning (such as drinking street water that has been contaminated by pesticides or antifreeze); attacks from other dogs; injuries from broken glass, jagged metal or wire; deliberate injuries from rock-, stick- or gun-wielding humans; exposure to disease; and much more. If your dog even looks like a potentially valuable purebred, it is at additional risk from dog thieves. A free-roaming dog is also subject to capture by animal control authorities; though this is a valuable community service, if you are a pet owner whose roaming dog is hauled off to the animal shelter, you have given yourself an unnecessary night of suffering by making the dog vulnerable to capture in the first place.

Appropriate confinement protects your dog from most of these hazards. The best form of confinement is a dogproof yard, with a fence that cannot be jumped or climbed or squeezed through. If your dog can scale high fences, consider adding a strip along the top that tilts inward, so that the dog cannot get over it. If the dog is a digger, you can sink your fence a foot or more into the ground, embed it in concrete, or lay an 18-inch strip of chicken wire along the ground at the base of the fence and cover it with a thick layer of gravel. Make sure that structures such as doghouses are not placed next to the fence, so that your dog cannot leap to the top of the doghouse and then jump over the fence itself. Make sure the yard has shade for the dog, water at all times, and toys to keep it entertained, and that you provide necessary social time so that the dog doesn't get bored.

Even in a secure yard, a dog is not necessarily safe from dognappers. It is a good idea to provide locks for your gates; if nothing else, a broken lock can elevate your missing dog from the status of "stray" to "stolen property" in the eyes of your local police department. However, it is an even better idea to keep your dog indoors when you are away from home.

Another good preventive measure is to become at least minimally acquainted with your neighbors and their pets, and to make sure they are familiar with yours. A neighbor who knows your dog by sight will realize something is wrong if he happens to see a stranger leading the dog down the street, or if he sees it running off with a group of strays. This can result in prompt action, which can make the difference between heartbreak and a happy reunion. If your dog has a habit of getting loose and visiting the neighbors for snacks, getting acquainted can prevent a well-intentioned adoption of this "stray," and give you a place to start your search if the dog should disappear.

To cats, most fences are just things to climb over and sit on, so a well-fenced yard is not the answer to keeping a cat protected. The best protection, of course, is to keep your cat indoors or in an escape-proof (i.e., roofed) enclosure at all times. This method is still controversial among cat owners; some feel it is cruel to keep a cat, which enjoys roaming by nature, confined in this way; others believe that exposing a cat to the hazards of the streets is even more cruel.

Free-roaming cats seem to be more vulnerable than roaming dogs to malicious humans—perhaps because a large dog inspires more respect, perhaps because cats roam into the fenced yards and territories of others. In my mother's neighborhood, more than 27 cats disappeared within a 3-block radius—and three of my mother's cats were among them. Many people dislike cats and may take drastic action against felines that dig up their flowerbeds or catch birds in their yards—or they may take action for perverse reasons beyond the comprehension of a pet lover. Cat traps, pellet guns and poison are all hazards a cat owner should be aware of when making the decision to let a cat roam. In addition, cat owners should keep in mind that, unlike dogs, cats are not particularly social animals, and an encounter between two strange cats is more likely to result in a potentially damaging fight than a friendship.

Whether you own dogs, cats or birds, proper identification is vital for their protection. Make sure your dogs wear current license and rabies tags. Birds should wear any appropriate bands. It's also an excellent idea to provide dogs and/or cats with identification tags that list an address and phone number, or the number of a pet recovery service. But keep in mind that collars and tags can be lost or removed; the best, most permanent form of identification is a simple, painless tattoo. Tattoos should be registered with an appropriate agency; then, if someone finds your pet, that person can call the registry, who can then contact you to make arrangements for the recovery of your pet. Shelters and veterinarians are familiar with these registries, and will know whom to contact if they find a tattooed pet; many research laboratories are becoming sensitized to tattoos also, and will contact the appropriate registry if a tattooed pet comes into their hands. In addition, a registered tattoo is a way of proving your ownership of an animal to the police or in court, should an ownership question arise.

According to the National Dog Registry, which registers pet tattoo numbers, pet losses are highest during the summer and during the holidays. These are times of outdoor activities, family visits and travel; if you make special plans during the summer or holidays, make sure these plans include pet safety.

If you lose a pet while traveling—from a relative's home, hotel, campground or rest stop—your frustration will be compounded by the fact that both you and your pet are in unfamiliar territory. All bets about where your pet would be "likely" to go are off. In some cases pets decide to head back home—even if home is 3,000 miles away. Others head for places that look like home; for example, one escaped bird was found at a house that had a car just like its owner's car in the driveway. A dog lost at a dog show headed from the center of a large town to the outskirts, miles away, and was found wandering in a more rural neighborhood that resembled its neighborhood at home.

For those who suspect that *Lassie Come Home* and *Incredible Journey* stories are just so much romantic fiction, I can attest from personal experience that they really happen! While traveling from our city home to our country cabin, one of our cats clawed her way through the screen window of the family camper and escaped from the moving car. We were certain that was the last of her—yet the next weekend she showed up at the cabin for dinner! We'll never know if she followed the familiar route by smell, or traveled across country in response to some mysterious magnetic guidance system.

If you travel with your pet, take precautions. Besides its regular ID tags, add a barrel tag that encloses a strip of paper on which you can write your "current" travel address—your hotel, the address of the person you are visiting, or the address of someone who can be contacted about your pet at any time. Make sure your pet doesn't roam freely in strange territory, and that its method of confinement—stake-out chain, exercise pen or crate—is secure. Don't leave your pet unattended in a campground or hotel room. If you are staying with friends or relatives, make sure your pet can stay in an area that is as dogproof as its yard at home, or provide some sort of secure wire exercise pen (these can be purchased with wire roofs for extra security) that will keep the dog safe. When you leave your friend's house, keep the pet confined to a room, basement or garage until you return.

Keep your pet—dog or cat—crated at night and when riding in the car. This not only prevents your pet from escaping, but protects it in case of an emergency or accident. If you should be involved in an accident, the crate will not only prevent your pet from being thrown around the car—which is hazardous not only to it but to you and your passengers—but also enable authorities to handle your pet safely and transport it to an animal shelter, where you or a friend can reclaim it.

If you decide not to take your pet traveling and leave it with a friend instead, make sure the friend's home and yard are as pet-proof as yours, and that your friend will observe your safety precautions about keeping the pet confined. Remember that your friend's home is in strange territory, so you don't want your pet to get loose. (One day a lovely cat showed up on our doorstep, yet its ID tag indicated that it lived miles away. Repeated calls to the number on the tag finally reunited the cat with its owner, who had left it with a petsitter in our neighborhood. The cat did not come to the petsitter when she called and searched for it, and had it not worn an ID tag, it might have ended up in a shelter.) And even if the pet finds its way back to its home, no one will be there to receive it.

If you leave your pet at home, make sure its caretaker is fully familiar with your safety requirements. Don't hire someone who will carelessly leave doors or gates open, or leave your dog in the yard all day unattended. Remember, too, that if your pet does escape, it may not come when a strange caretaker calls, so try to make sure it and your caretaker are on good terms before you leave.

The holiday season presents the same travel dangers as summer. Even if you don't travel during the holidays, there are some special precautions you should take. If friends and relatives visit you, make sure they will be responsible about keeping doors and gates shut; this rule should be especially firmly impressed upon children. Pay attention to how your guests are getting along with your pets; you don't want your cat taking the first open window or door available to it in a desperate attempt to escape a teasing child. If you have a party, keep your pets confined in a room so that they cannot slip out while guests are being greeted or saying their farewells in an open doorway. Remember that the comings and goings of the holiday season—irregular hours, parties, guests, carolers, trees in the house (always mystifying to pets), and frequent changes of routine—can be disrupting or upsetting to pets. You need to be especially aware of their safety and well-being at this time, and make sure that you don't get so caught up in the festivities that you ignore or overlook the needs of these special family members.

Emergencies and Disasters

In light of the significant disasters that have occurred throughout the U.S. in the past few years—floods in the Midwest, hurricanes in the south, fires and earthquakes in Los Angeles—it seems appropriate to discuss ways to make sure that, should such a disaster strike your home, you don't lose your pet. Nothing can completely guarantee that, in the case of a significant disaster or fire, you will be able to save or retrieve your pets, but you *can* take steps to improve their chances of survival and recovery.

In the case of the Los Angeles earthquake of January 1994, the most significant number of pet casualties were probably outdoor pets. Many panicky pets raced into the unlit streets and were struck by cars. While some of these pets may have escaped from indoors, it is likely that many more were outdoor animals to begin with. Thus, the first step you can take to help ensure your pet's safety in an emergency is to keep it indoors as much as possible, especially at night.

Keeping your pet indoors is only the first step, however. A well-disciplined and obedient pet stands a much greater chance of survival than one that is accustomed to ignoring you and your commands. A pet that is trained to obey your voice commands can not only be controlled, but has something to respond to other than its own terrified panic. Every dog should be trained in the basics: Come, Sit, and Stay. You want to be certain that your pet will come to you when you call, *every* time you call, and will stay with you when you tell it to. (It's a good idea to train pets in the presence of distractions, so that you can teach them to come to you even when something more interesting, or frightening, is going on nearby.)

Cats are less easy to train and discipline, as every cat owner knows, but it is helpful to make sure that your cats know and respond to their names, or to a particular call-word (such as "kitty kitty kitty"). Many people believe that it's useless to even try to train a cat, so they don't try—yet with patience and love, cats *can* be trained.

You can greatly increase your pet's safety by teaching it to enter a crate on command. To do this, you must teach the pet to associate crates primarily with positive experiences, like rewards (petting, praise, and treats) rather than only negative experiences (such as trips to the veterinarian).

Many pet owners teach their dogs to sleep in their crates; my sister's dogs respond enthusiastically to the command "Crate!" and leap into their respective "dens," waiting eagerly for their bedtime snack. Cats, too, can be taught to consider a crate a safe retreat, which will improve their chances of choosing a crate to hide in should the earth start to move.

Knowing your pet's habits also helps. Observe them when they are frightened: How do they respond? Where do they go? I had no fears for my cats during the earthquake, because I already knew that at the first tremor, they would race under the bed—the safest place they could possibly be. Nor would they come out until they were convinced that all was secure. If I had needed to retrieve them, I would have known where to look; in the meantime, I did not have to worry about their safety at the risk of my own.

This is an important issue. One pet owner in our building was badly bruised when furniture fell on her while she was trying to locate her cat—which, like mine, had wisely taken shelter. If a disaster strikes, please, no matter how much you love your pets, see to the safety of yourself and your family *first*. When you are safe and the immediate danger is over, you will be able to go back and retrieve your pets. Remember, if something happens to you and you are hospitalized (or worse), no one will be able to recover or protect your pets!

After the initial emergency is over, you may still need to take steps to ensure your pets' safety, especially if you are forced to evacuate your home. If you have to take refuge in a makeshift shelter, you may not be able to keep your pets with you, or you may have to keep them outside. Following are some steps you can take to ensure their safety:

• A crate provides the best security and protection. Temporary disaster shelters are less likely to be concerned about accepting a pet that is securely confined. Make sure you have enough crates of sufficient size to accommodate all your pets. Keep them readily available. Be sure the doors are in good working order; older crate doors tend to rust and stick.

• The second-best form of security is a leash. Securing your pet's leash to a harness rather than a collar is safer for the pet and provides you with greater control, especially for cats. Accustom all pets, including cats (yes, cats *can* be leash-trained) to the use of a leash and harness. Again, make sure your pets associate leashes with positive experiences.

• If you have neither a crate nor a leash handy (or no time to grab either), some professionals recommend putting a cat or a small dog into a pillowcase and tying the case shut. The pet isn't going to like it, but it will be safe, it can breathe, and you can carry it.

• Make sure all your pets have some form of identification, such as collar tags or tattoos. Anyone can read a tag, and it provides valuable information should your pet be picked up by animal regulation authorities. It also provides you with proof of ownership.

• Keep a pet emergency kit handy. This kit should include food, water, a dish, an extra collar or harness and leash, a supply of any medication the pet requires, and some basic first aid supplies. Include a copy of your pet's vaccination records; a disaster shelter may require proof of vaccination. If you include canned food, don't forget a can opener; however, dry food is preferable because it is lighter, more easily measured out, and doesn't have to be refrigerated. For warmth, include a pet sweater or blanket; lightweight aluminum emergency blankets are also available. Keep your kit light; if you have a large dog who can carry a backpack, why not convert the pack into a doggie emergency kit?

Remember, preparation is your best defense. A major emergency may never happen to you, but it is far better to be prepared for an event that never occurs, than to be caught without resources when an unexpected disaster strikes.

Recovery

If, in spite of your precautions, your pet disappears, prompt action is vitally important. The following steps should be followed carefully and diligently.

1. Search your neighborhood. As soon as you are aware of your pet's absence, walk through your neighborhood calling the pet's name and looking for it. If your pet has favorite haunts, check those first. Methodically comb an area of several blocks; remember that pets often travel through yards, so they can cover a lot of territory quickly. Keep your eyes open for anything unusual: a pack of dogs in the distance, a van you've never seen before, evidence of a dog- or cat-fight, and so forth. Check under cars and bushes. If your dog normally comes running to the sound of a fork on a dinner dish, or your cat to the rattle of a kibble-box, take these items with you to reinforce your calling. This is no time to be shy: If you meet a neighbor or delivery person while searching, ask if that person has seen your pet.

2. Extend your search. If an immediate search of your neighborhood doesn't turn up any sign of your pet, and it hasn't returned home in the meantime, it's time to search a larger area by car. It's best to make this a two-person effort: one to drive, one to watch and call for the pet. Again, remember that your pet can cover a considerable distance in a short time. Drive slowly, and do a block-by-block grid search of the area.

3. Contact your local animal control office. If your pet has a city or county license tag (and it's wise to make sure it does beforehand!), the animal control office may contact you if it is located. However, if your pet has been missing for 24 hours or overnight, don't wait for a call: Contact the authorities yourself. Remember, the pet's collar and tags may have been removed or lost. If you have evidence that your pet was stolen, such as a broken lock, a severed collar or chain, or a damaged fence, contact these authorities immediately, and also notify your police department. Provide the office with a clear description of your pet—breed, sex, color, size, identifying marks or tattoos, whether or not it was wearing a collar, and its name. It's a good idea to keep some clear, recent color prints of your pet on hand so that you can take one of these to your animal control office.

It's a good idea to know whom to call about lost pets before it happens to you. In some cases the animal control office is associated with the police department; in others it may be a part of the city offices; in others the function may be handled by a local animal shelter or humane organization. In some areas, one office may handle strays while another handles the pickup of dead animals. Be sure to ask about both.

It won't hurt to report your loss to the police department, but don't count on much help either—unless, as I said earlier, you have evidence of theft and/or break-in. If a significant amount of pet theft has been going on in your area, your police department can let you know, and your report may be helpful in the case. However, lost pets are usually a low priority for police departments, which are universally underbudgeted and overworked. In some cases, a sympathetic department will at least agree to keep its eyes open on the streets for your pets; this is more likely in a small town or neighborhood with a low volume of crime than in a big city.

4. Contact animal shelters. You should start checking with animal shelters, pounds, humane associations, benevolent associations and any other place you can think of that takes in stray pets, between 24 and 48 hours after your pet disappears. Again, provide a clear description of the pet, including any identification it may have. Ask about strays and dead animals.

In large urban areas, shelters may handle so many animals that they are unable to answer questions about specific pets over the phone, insisting instead that you come down in person to look for your pet. If this is the case, visit daily. Most public shelters can only keep an animal for a few days, after which it is put up for adoption or destroyed.

Check with *all* the shelters in your vicinity. If you live close to a county line or a city boundary, check with shelters in the next county or town. When we picked up a stray dog near our own neighborhood, we didn't realize we'd crossed a county line in the process—so the dog went to the shelter in that county, miles from where it had been found, rather than to the nearby shelter in our own county. When you contact a shelter, be sure to ask the person you speak to what other shelters you should contact.

In the case of an emergency, be aware that your local shelter may be damaged, or that it may have an overflow and have to send some pets to other nearby shelters. Find out where pets that would normally be handled by that shelter have gone. And try not to worry: Los Angeles area shelters were aware of the unusual circumstances involved in the 1994 quake, and kept pets far beyond the usual time limits before offering them for adoption, making every effort to locate their owners. Some even provided shelter for pets whose owners were left temporarily homeless.

5. Start a poster campaign. If your pet has been missing for 24 hours, it's time to start putting up "lost pet" signs. The best method is to draw up a clear, darkly lettered sign with the appropriate information, and have several hundred copies run off at your local quick-print shop. Be sure to include as much of the following information as is appropriate in your situation:

• Type of animal lost (dog, cat, bird).

• Breed (St. Bernard, Siamese, Cockatoo).

• Brief description ("small brown female dog with red collar" or "black and white neutered male cat with green eyes"). Remember that many people aren't familiar with specific breeds, so describing your pet simply as a "Shih Tzu" may not be sufficient.

• The pet's name, especially if it appears on the pet's identification tag. (Remember, however, that pets often won't respond to their names when they are upset or when the caller is a stranger.)

• The general area from which the pet disappeared ("Lost near the intersection of Oak and Vine").

• A phone number that will be answered at any time of day. If you plan to be searching for your pet, list a friend's number, or make sure someone can monitor your phone at all times. At the very least, have an answering machine!

• Identification information: The words "tattooed, registered dog" might prompt a dognapper to return your property for a reward, rather than risk trying to sell it.

• **REWARD**. Don't specify an amount, but do offer a reward. This added incentive has brought many a pet home.

• A photo, if you have one that will reproduce well.

Make sure the words "Lost Dog/Cat" and "Reward" are clearly visible from a distance. These signs should be posted where they can be read from the street, so the most important part of the message should be the most prominent. If a person is interested in the rest of your message, he will return for another look.

Post your signs throughout your own neighborhood, and on major streets and intersections. Be sure to hit all four corners of an intersection, so that people can see them no matter which direction they're coming from. Check your signs often to make sure they are still in place and legible; a rainstorm could mean that you have to replace them all.

Post your signs in veterinary offices, pet shops, grooming shops, shelters, laundromats, grocery stores and anywhere else you think they'll attract attention. The more exposure you give to your campaign, the more likely you are to get a lead. For example, a well-meaning pet lover might have found your injured pet and taken it to a veterinarian; if every vet in your area knows about your loss, and the signs are posted in the waiting area, a reunion is more likely.

6. Advertise. Put a notice in the lost and found section of your local newspaper, or in several local papers. List a brief description of the pet (Lost: 3-year-old female Airedale), a number that can be reached at any time, and the word "REWARD." When the ad appears, check it for accuracy. Don't stop there: Check the papers every day for notices under the "found" section, too.

7. Talk to your neighbors. You should start on this no later than 24 hours after your loss. Go from door to door, asking your neighbors if they have seen your pet. Carry a photo of the animal with you. If no one is home, leave one of your "Lost" posters on the doorstep. Be friendly and helpful; apologize for disturbing the neighbors, but make sure they see the picture and know where to contact you. You might want to leave one of your posters with each person you speak to. Ask, too, if they have noticed anything unusual in the neighborhood around the time your pet disappeared—did they notice strangers who appeared to be "casing" the neighborhood? A strange van or truck cruising the streets slowly, or coming

back to the area several times? A pack of stray dogs that your
dog might have run off with? If your dog or cat is an unneutered
male, ask if they know of a female in the neighborhood who is
in season and attracting suitors; your pet might have joined
the crowd. On your trip through the neighborhood, be sure to
talk to regular delivery people: the mail carrier, paper carrier, milk deliverer, or anyone else who is frequently in the
neighborhood. Often these people are very familiar with the
neighborhood pets, and as they often travel through a neighborhood on foot, they see more of what goes on in the area
than most of us. Give each of them a copy of the picture of
your pet—with your name, address and phone number on the
back—that they can post in their delivery trucks.

8. Contact appropriate registries. If your pet has a tattoo or tag that is registered with a pet recovery service or
tattoo registry, notify the agency about your loss. This way,
your dog or cat will be put on their list of lost pets. If anyone
calls in with your pet's tag or tattoo number, the registry will
call you. Many registries also offer additional services, such
as alternate numbers that can be called in case you're not
home. Or, you can authorize some registries to advance the
finder of your pet sufficient funds to place the pet in a boarding kennel or shelter until you can pick it up.

9. Follow up all leads. Whenever someone calls you with
a tip or a sighting, follow it up, even if it seems unlikely. Dogs
and cats can travel tremendous distances in a short amount
of time. Many pet owners have said that the only thing that
brought their pets home was tracking down every lead until
they hit the right one.

However, be cautious. There are, sad to say, people who
make a living exploiting grieving pet owners. Never give anyone money until you have your pet in hand. If a person says
he will meet you somewhere and to bring your reward along,
make sure the "somewhere" is safe. If a person says "give me
the money and I'll go get your pet," tell that person he will get
the money when you have the pet and have identified it as
your own. Don't be taken in by the fact that the person has
given a detailed, accurate description of your pet, even one
that includes items you didn't mention in your ad or poster.
The person might have seen your pet, or even had it in his

possession and sold it to someone else, and be hoping to collect double for it. If you do get ripped off, be sure to report the incident; it may not be the only such incident, and your description may help the police track down the person.

10. Be persistent. Keep looking. Go back to your neighbors and delivery people; check back with the animal control office and shelters; check with the police and ask to speak to the officer handling your case. Check your posters and make sure they are still up and visible. Continue to run ads. Continue to search. As time goes by, your chances of finding your pet become increasingly remote, but through persistence and luck, amazing recoveries have occurred weeks, months and even years later.

When should you stop looking? I wish I could give a precise cut-off point, but I can't. I've known cats to come home after absences of three days to a week, and others to disappear without a trace. I know people who haven't given up the search after several years. However, I would suggest that you be realistic. If your pet has not been located (dead or alive) after several weeks, and no one has responded to your ads or signs, you may consider making the decision that your pet is truly gone—even if you continue the search.

At this time, it would be healthiest for you to begin working through the bereavement process just as if you knew the pet was dead. You might wish to conduct a eulogy or memorial service for your pet to give you and your family that separation ritual many pet owners have found helpful.

And if, months later, after you've worked through your grief and moved on, a scruffy stray that looks just like Precious shows up on your doorstep, and you check its tattoo and realize that by some miracle it *is* Precious—what joy! It can happen, and has happened. But it is far better to accept your loss and learn to deal with it, only to be delightfully surprised by an unexpected return, than to spend months or years refusing to accept the loss and waiting for a return that never comes.

Chapter 9

Where There's
A Will...

DEATH IS INEVITABLE FOR OUR PETS, and the average person is likely to outlive several pets in the course of a lifetime. But death is also inevitable for pet owners. Death comes as the natural consequence of a long life, but it can also come suddenly and unexpectedly, through accident or illness, to any one of us.

As a responsible pet owner, it is important to be prepared not only for your pet's death, but for the consequences your own death will have on any pets that survive you. If you have made no arrangements for the care of surviving pets, your death *could* be a death sentence to them, as well. This chapter describes some arrangements you can make to protect your pets and make sure your wishes regarding their welfare are carried out, should you no longer be around to care for them.

Death isn't the only thing you need to prepare for. An accident or extended illness could also rob your pets of their caretaker, perhaps for months, perhaps permanently. If you face a lengthy hospitalization, or must move to a caregiving facility that does not allow pets, it will be of great comfort to know that your animals will still be cared for as you would wish.

Before we get into the legal aspects of providing for your

pets, I'd like to point out the single most important thing you need to do to ensure their safety—whether or not you choose to take any of the other steps described in this chapter. That is to make sure that someone can take charge of your pets, even temporarily, at any time. This is particularly important if you live alone. Otherwise, should you be involved in an accident while away from home, no one will know that you have animals at home that need to be fed and cared for!

In the event of your death, you don't want to take a chance of having your animals forgotten until executors or other officials arrive at your home days later. It's also possible for a pet to be overlooked and forgotten in the confusion of handling a person's final affairs. If no one knows you have a cat, for example, the frightened animal might hide somewhere while strangers "invade" your home, and not be discovered until too late. In addition, if you have made no arrangements to have someone care for your pet, then, when it is discovered, in most cases it will be taken to the nearest city or county animal shelter and be at the mercy of whatever adoption and/or disposal program is in use there.

You can take several steps to protect your pets from this kind of disaster. The first is to carry a wallet alert card that lists the name and phone number of someone who can come and care for your pets. Even a neighbor who will agree to come in and provide fresh food and water before a more permanent caretaker can be found is better than nothing! (Make sure this neighbor knows whom to contact for permanent care, however.) Your caretaker should have access to your pets, and should know how many pets you have and of what kind, where they are located, their names, and the name and number of your veterinarian.

The second step you can take is to post "Pet Inside" stickers on doors or windows where rescue or medical personnel are likely to enter your home in the event of an emergency. Be sure you note how many pets you have, and what type; if all your sticker says is "Pet inside," and firemen rescue one dog, they won't know to look for the two cats and the parakeet. You might wish to place an "in case of emergency, contact…" notice on the inside of your front and back doors, so that these same rescue personnel will know where to take your pets.

Some animal shelters provide stickers that inform rescuers that your pets are to be brought to that particular shelter for care; then, if you have made prior arrangements with the shelter, it will contact your pet caretakers and make sure your pets are properly cared for.

Wills and Codicils

The law considers your pets to be property, just like your silverware and your sofa. Since a will is the most formal and legally binding declaration of your intentions regarding the distribution of your property after you die, you owe it to your pets to make sure they are included in this vital document.

However, despite the importance of a complete and properly prepared will, this is not the most important document as far as your pets are concerned, nor is it even the place to spell out specific arrangements for the care of your pet. One problem with a will is that it is generally not read until several days after the death of its author. You will want your pets to be in the hands of their new caretaker well before then! If any legal disputes arise over the will, the final settlement of property can drag on for months or years.

The solution is to prepare a statement of intent that establishes a guardianship for your pets, which is kept as a separate codicil to your will. A codicil is an amendment to a will and is usually used for minor changes or for matters that may have to be updated frequently. It can be brief and doesn't involve as complex a legal process as a will; thus, it is easier to keep current, which is important because you'll need to update it every time you add or lose a pet or change your designated guardian. Like a will, however, a codicil must be witnessed by two people, and a copy should be stapled to every copy of your will.

Lawyers often add a phrase to codicils that indicates that the codicil does not affect any portion of your will but the part you are discussing. That statement might read, "In all other respects, I confirm and republish my will." The codicil should also refer to the date of your current will (as in "this is a codicil to my will dated March 7, 1990").

Though your codicil needs to be attached to your will, keep in mind that this is a statement of intent that should be acted upon immediately after your death. It should be easy to locate, so that whoever handles your affairs upon your death can find it without delay. You may even wish to leave a copy of the codicil with the person you designate as your pets' guardian, so that person can legally take over your pets right away.

Your statement of intent should inform the executor of your estate of the name of the person selected to take care of your pet(s), and the names and general descriptions of the pets involved. For this statement to hold up in court, you need to "bequeath" your pets to the guardian in return for a specific amount of money. The money is paid into your estate by the guardian in "compensation" for the "value" of the pets; however, it can be a nominal amount. Your statement might read:

"I bequeath my dogs, Peppy and Marjie, to my sister, Sarah Doe, in return for the sum of One Dollar. Sarah Doe will act as the guardian for my dogs and will provide for their care and maintenance as follows..."

You can then specify what you want Sarah Doe to do with your pets: Do you expect her to keep them, or do you simply want her to find good homes for them? Do you want your pets to be euthanized? The statement is not the place to spell out feeding and care instructions or details of how you want your pets' guardian to carry out your instructions.

Your codicil should be updated as often as necessary to reflect changes in your situation. For example, if you make a will at age 30 and live to be 70, the pets you've described in the original codicil will have passed on long ago. It's also possible that sister Sarah has passed on, or that changes in her own life have made it impossible for her to accept your pets now. An outdated statement of intent can create more problems than it solves.

Whenever one of your pets dies or you adopt a new pet, rewrite your codicil to reflect the change. If you move, or break off relations with the friend or relative you had hoped would take your pets, or if that person dies or is otherwise unable to fulfill the role of guardian, you should select a new guardian and rewrite the statement to reflect that change. By keeping this information in the codicil and not in the will itself, you won't have to rewrite your will every time you get a new pet.

Does this mean that you don't even have to think about

pets when you write your will? No. The purpose of a codicil is to establish a guardianship so that your intentions regarding your pets can be acted upon immediately. In your will you can specify something very important: the portion of your estate that will go toward the care of your pets. For example, Sarah Doe may be happy to take on Peppy and Marjie, but does she have the money to provide for them? Does she want to be responsible for their feeding, vet care and other needs for the next several years? If this is an important concern for your chosen guardian, consider providing funds in your will to handle the costs of caring for your surviving pets.

The most common method of doing this is to use your will to set up a trust fund for the guardian to draw upon for the care of the pets. This trust should be bequeathed to the guardian, not to the pets themselves. Your guardian and your pets will experience far fewer legal hassles if you leave your money to a human (or to an appropriate organization) rather than to your animals. You can also make gifts to the guardian(s) through your will, and you can even specify that the gifts be withdrawn if there is evidence that your chosen guardian is not caring for your pets as stipulated.

The executor of your will can control the disposition of your personal property, including pets, for a six-month claim period, during which time he can monitor the care your animals are receiving. D.E. of Georgia, for example, has "provided life maintenance money to be distributed to a suitable new owner by the executor of the estate. The new owner will not get the money directly; bills will be submitted as proof of care and the executor will pay them directly to the provider. In that way, should the pets be old or have health problems, they would not be a financial burden to the new owner. We have set down criteria for a new owner, but one can only hope that he or she will love our pets as much as we do."

Pet owners have made a variety of plans for funding the care of their pets. One had made her daughter the beneficiary of her $7,000 IRA, which was to be used specifically for the care of her pets. Any money remaining that did not go to pet care was to be donated to an SPCA. Another hopes to ensure that her house is paid for and that enough money remains to take care of the pets without moving or separating them. Another family has established a savings account on which their sons could draw to fund the care of the surviving pets, should both husband and wife die at the same time. Some have made arrangements through their wills; others have made financial arrangements outside of their wills.

Another option is to leave a large bequest to a local humane society or other charitable organization that is involved with animals. This organization can be designated as the financial caretaker for your pets, and you may choose to make that organization responsible for providing them with appropriate homes as well as for their expenses. Upon the death of your pet(s), the remainder of your bequest can then be used by the organization to help all pets—a good legacy for a caring pet owner! (It is not unheard of for a person to specify that they would prefer mourners to make donations to a favorite animal-related charity rather than send flowers.) Even if you don't wish to designate a local charity as the caretaker for your pets, it is good to keep in mind that there are a number of worthwhile organizations and research projects dedicated to the health and well-being of pets that are worth remembering when drawing up a will.

Keep in mind that wills *can* be broken, particularly if you make "unreasonable" bequests or demands. For example, if you leave the bulk of a rich estate to Rover or Pussums, and token amounts to a variety of relatives, it's not unlikely that your relatives will contest the will. It's also not unlikely that they will win, and the fate of your pets will then depend on a court decision or the mercy of those relatives. A relative who is well provided for is less likely to successfully contest a "reasonable" bequest of a few thousand dollars to your pets or their caretaker.

If you wish to exclude claimants to your estate in favor of your pets, do so by mentioning every possible claimant by name and stating that you specifically wish to exclude them, or leave them token amounts. If you have strong reasons for your exclusions, state them (for example, *"I do not wish my son, David Doe, to inherit any of my estate, because he has failed to contact me for the last 10 years."*) It is far more difficult for a relative to contest a will if he is actually written out of it, than if he can claim to have been "forgotten."

Your lawyer can give you more specific advice on how to make bequests for pet care and assign guardianships in a codicil. Your lawyer can also advise you on how the laws in your state affect your desires regarding the care of your pets.

Finding the Right Guardian

Who is the best person to take care of your pets? You may have many options to choose from, and there may be a few that you didn't think of.

If you are married, you will probably expect your spouse to take over the care of the family pets if you die, and vice versa. In many states, community property laws make this automatic. In that case, you may wish to make more specific guardianship arrangements in case both you and your spouse die at the same time.

A spouse may not always be the best choice, however. You may not wish to leave your pets in the care of a spouse with whom you do not have a good relationship, or one from whom you are separated but who might still inherit your pets under community property laws. If your spouse loathes pets or is allergic to them, and only tolerates them for your sake, the most you can expect is for this person to find new homes for the pets as soon as possible. If you have any doubts about whether your spouse will follow your wishes, select another guardian, or make sure that these wishes are clearly spelled out in your codicil—for example, that the spouse is *not* to turn the pets over to an animal shelter or have them euthanized.

If you are unmarried but living with a "significant other," in most cases community property laws do not apply to your relationship. If you have established a common-law marriage, your "spouse" may inherit your pets and other property, but it would be wise to check on the legal details of this status in your state—and far wiser to make written legal arrangements. Many cases have arisen lately in which relatives have contested the right of a "significant other" to inherit a lover's property, even when a will has been drawn up to that effect. So if there is any possibility of question in your relationship, you would do well to secure the fate of your pets—and your "other"—legally. In any case, the same considerations apply to an "other" as to a spouse: Do not bequeath your pets to this person if you cannot reasonably expect the individual to provide for them as you would wish.

The next logical choice for guardianship is one or more close relatives: your children, parents, brothers or sisters. Don't overlook more distant relatives and in-laws as you consider your choice. Different relatives may be appropriate guardians for different pets. For example, your daughter may want to keep the dog she grew up with, while your sister may be particularly fond of one of your cats. Be sure to consider the living situation of the relative of choice: It may not be reasonable to expect your 70-year-old mother to care for your 2-year-old Doberman. If your children are young adults living in apartments and holding down full-time jobs, they, too, may have trouble accommodating large, active dogs. You may have to accept the fact that such family members may be able to act only as guardians who will be responsible for finding appropriate homes for your pets.

The next choice on the list is a good friend. Obviously, you will want this friend to be a person who loves, understands and knows how to care for pets—and the same conditions regarding situation and lifestyle apply to your friends as to your family members. After close friends come more distant friends, coworkers, neighbors, etc. The less close a person is to your pet, the more likely that this guardianship will extend only to finding good homes for your pets, and your guardians may insist that a reasonable time-limit be imposed on their guardianship—i.e., if they are unable to locate appropriate homes for your pets within a certain amount of time, they are free to make other arrangements.

If your designated guardians do not intend to keep your pets, you and they should be aware of some of the options that may be available to them in their search for such homes. More options are available to owners of purebreds than to owners of mixed-breed pets.

If you purchased a purebred dog or cat from a breeder, that breeder may be the best contact for placing the pet after you die. Many breeders stipulate that if you can't keep the pet for any reason, you are required to return it, so that the breeder can find another home for it. If your pet is difficult to place because of age or illness, the breeder will often decide to keep it himself. If you co-own a pet with a breeder or anyone else, the co-owner is as much the pet's legal owner as you are, and the pet should go to that person.

If you own a purebred dog, a breed rescue service may be able to help you or your guardian find a new home for it. Rescue services were developed to literally "rescue" dogs that have been abandoned or mistreated by their owners, and exist for many breeds. Many have arrangements with local shelters to adopt any dogs of their breed that are brought in. A few rescues also handle mixed-breeds that contain a large percentage of their target breed; thus, if you have a Doberman/Rottweiler cross, you might be able to turn to either a Doberman rescue or a Rottweiler rescue. Usually the service will place the dog in a foster home until a permanent home can be found. Rescues are generally shoe-string operations, funded by the generosity and love of their members, who often feed, care and pay all expenses for the dogs out of their own pocket. Thus, if you do want the help of such a service, making some financial arrangement to fund the care of your dog will be most welcome and appropriate.

The best way to locate a breed rescue is to contact the national breed club for your breed. However, not all national clubs are aware of all the rescues in operation, so it's a good idea to check with local breed clubs or local pet care professionals if your national club can't help you.

If you are part of the showing and/or breeding world, other people interested in your breed may be willing to take over the care of your animals, especially if they are successful in the show ring or have produced quality offspring. If you know of breeders or exhibitors who might be interested in your animals, make a list of them and keep it with your codicil, so that your executor can contact them as soon as possible. If you know that certain individuals will be interested in specific animals, make sure this information is also available to your executor or temporary guardian.

A final alternative is to designate a pet care professional such as your veterinarian to act as a guardian until your pet can be placed in a new home. You might wish to stipulate in your codicil that your pet is to be boarded at a particular clinic or boarding facility until a new home is found. Make sure

that the veterinarian or facility you choose is willing to agree
to this arrangement, and that your will and/or statement of
intent provides sufficient funds for it.

Euthanasia

It is not uncommon for a pet owner to write into his or her
will that any surviving pets be euthanized after the owner's
death. Some pet owners choose this option because they have
been unable to find appropriate guardians for their pets; others are simply unaware of the alternatives available. Some
make this decision to ensure that their pets will never be
abused or uncared for; others believe that no one else can
provide the same love and care for their pets that they did, or
that their pets could never be happy in another home.

"If I could not make prior arrangements with someone to
take the pets, I would have them put to sleep as part of my
last will and testament," wrote Rosemary S. of California.
"Animals have been known to mourn and search for deceased
masters. It would be a tragedy to have animals that were
once loved and cared for left alone and uncared for, to starve,
be killed or abused for painful, inhuman laboratory testing."

"When I first made my will 20 years ago, I thought it best
to request that the three dogs I then had be put down, as I did
not want them to go to strangers or to the pound," wrote Helen
B. of New York. Patricia B. of Ohio agreed: "If they can't be
taken into a relative's home, they are to be put to sleep; I
would never put them in an animal shelter." And Deborah C.
of Pennsylvania said, "If my parents are no longer alive or
able to take care of her, she will be put to sleep and buried
with me in our mausoleum."

Specifying euthanasia for your pets in your will is not a
decision to be made lightly, however, even if you have the best
possible motives. It is a decision that may not sit well with
the legal authorities who handle your will, or with your remaining, possibly pet-loving, beneficiaries. In a highly publi-
cized case in San Francisco, for example, a widow requested
in her will that her dog be euthanized. Animal lovers raised
considerable public outcry, and the end result was that "Sido"
was spared. The dog was finally adopted by a member of the
San Francisco SPCA, became the SPCA's unofficial mascot,

and lived several happy years with his new owner until his death in 1986. This case established a precedent for the possible overturning of such a stipulation.

Sido was a young, healthy dog, and animal lovers felt that there was no just cause to deprive this dog of his life. Sido was also lucky to become the focus of a battle in California, where such issues often command considerable attention. He was equally fortunate to have been advocated by the San Francisco SPCA, an active SPCA with a strong commitment to saving pets' lives—and he was fortunate to have a chance at a new home through an SPCA member. Dogs and cats in other parts of the country may not be so fortunate. However, the case serves as a caution against inserting such a request into a will without good cause. Before you make such a stipulation, it is wise to investigate every possible alternative.

That doesn't mean that you should not seek to have a pet euthanized under any circumstances. In some cases, this may truly be the best alternative from the standpoint of the pet's well-being. If you have a pet that is very old or requires extensive medical care, it might not be fair either to the pet or to your designated guardian to insist that it be cared for indefinitely. The question to consider is how the pet's quality of life will be affected by your death. Cathy W. of California has made that decision for one of her pets:

"We have made arrangements that our 16-year-old Lhasa Apso be put to sleep. My parents would take our Toy Poodle and find homes for our other pets. We feel that our Lhasa would have a hard time adjusting to a new home, and she has a lot of medical problems that require daily medication."

Another case in which euthanasia might be a reasonable option is when a pet truly cannot adapt to another owner. Some pets are truly "one-person" animals—though such a determination should be made on a very realistic analysis of a pet's behavior. Guard against statements such as "Oh, Fifikins could never get along with anyone but me; no one else could understand her!" A dog who tends to ignore visitors might still adapt to a new owner; one who lunges viciously at everyone, however, may not be a good candidate for adoption. A formerly feral animal may also have difficulty adapting to a new owner. You may still be able to find someone who is willing to invest time and effort into giving your "impossible" pet a good home, however, so don't give up without looking.

No matter how you choose to provide for your pet in your will, you'll undoubtedly seek to make the decision that will be best for the well-being of your pet. Whether you choose to have your pet euthanized, or establish a private home for it with a huge financial endowment, it's important to make your decision with care, so that no one will be tempted to disagree with it after you're gone.

Documentation

Establishing a will and codicil is only part of what you need to do to make sure your pets are properly taken care of. It's very important to gather together all the papers pertaining to your pets and make sure they are in a place where your guardian or executor can locate them easily; you might even wish to leave duplicate copies with the guardian.

These papers may change over time as you lose old pets and gain new ones, so be sure to keep them updated. You don't want to add the confusion of trying to track down a pet that no longer exists to the problems of administering your estate. Among these papers, you should include:

1. Vital statistics. Your pet papers should include a descriptive list of all the pets you own. It is vital that you keep this list current, adding new pets as you acquire them, and noting whenever you "lose" a pet—whether it dies or you sell it or give it away. A good method for this is to maintain a logbook. In your log, you should record the following information for each animal:

• Species (cat, dog, bird, horse).

• Breed (Siamese, St. Bernard, Parrot, Appaloosa).

• Name—both the registered name, if any (e.g., Champion Happy Acres Rovalot of Thornhill) and the call name ("Rover").

• Sex, and whether or not the animal is altered.

• Birth date, or your best guess of the pet's age.

• Brief description: "Small tan short-haired dog with black patch on the side and white-tipped tail." Remember that the officials who handle your affairs may not know the difference between a Dandy Dinmont Terrier and a Bouvier des Flandres, or between a Himalayan and a Sphinx, so it's not a bad idea to provide a description of purebred pets as well.

• Identification numbers: registration numbers, city or county license numbers, tattoo numbers and their location on the animal, brands, bands, etc.

• Specific identifying marks: one-eared cat, eyes of different colors, unusual markings, prominent scars.

• Co-ownership information, if any, along with the names and addresses of co-owners.

• Championship information, if any.

• Location, if your animal is not at home—for example, if your dog is living with a handler or trainer, or your horse is at a commercial stable.

• A recent, clear, color photo of the pet that can aid in its identification. If your pet has any special identifying markings or scars, be sure the photograph shows them.

2. Identification. It is important for your guardian to be able to identify your pets and distinguish them from one another. If you have two black cats who look exactly alike, you might want to make sure that they wear collars of different colors, at least. If you have only one pet, or very different pets, visual identification is not such a problem.

If for any reason you fear that the ownership of your pets might be questioned in court—for instance, if you have an animal of value that someone might wish to claim—it's wise to have further proof of the animal's identification. This will also be helpful if you have many animals that look alike—for instance, if you operate a kennel or cattery—and you want to make certain that specific animals go to specific new owners. Your temporary guardian or executor may not be able to distinguish one animal from another, making a more indisputable form of identification vital. For dogs and cats, the best formal and legally verifiable means of identification is a tattoo number, registered with an appropriate agency. Tattooing is a quick and painless process, and provides a permanent form of identification that cannot be removed, as a tag can.

If your pet is a registered purebred, record its registration number in your log. Record any license and tag numbers, or rabies vaccination numbers. If you own birds, record any appropriate band information; if you own horses, record brands, tattoos, or whatever other form of identification you use.

3. Proof of ownership. Your records of identification are probably your best proof of ownership. Keep on file any appropriate registration papers showing transfer of ownership from a breeder or previous owner, as well as any bills of sale from pet shops or other sources. A scrapbook of photographs can also demonstrate ownership (through proof of possession).

If you co-own your pets with other parties, these co-owners will generally become the legal owners of your animals should you die. This is a situation in which proper identification is particularly important: If the animal has lived with you, its co-owner may not be able to distinguish it from other similar animals (for instance, a co-owner might not be able to pick out *his* St. Bernard from a kennel full of St. Bernards). Tags, tattoos or other forms of positive identification should be recorded so that the co-owner and your guardian and/or executor can make sure the right animals go to the right people. Make sure the temporary guardian of your animals can find the address and phone number of any and all co-owners, along with the name, description and identification of the co-owned animals.

Make sure your pets are licensed (licenses are required for dogs in most areas and for cats in some cities) and that the license records are included in your identification file. Matching licenses with license tags can help identify your pets.

4. Pedigrees. If your pet has a career as a show animal or is part of a breeding program, its guardian may wish to continue with that career. In addition, if a breeder agrees to take back an animal, he will want the pet's papers as well. Keep the pedigrees of your pets along with the rest of their important papers. If your pet has a record of show wins that would be important to its new owner, this can go with the pedigree.

5. Medical records. The more health problems your pet has, the more important complete medical records are. Your pet's new owner will need to know what medications, if any, your pet requires, the status of its vaccinations, whether or not it is on a special diet, and whether there are any particular recurring health problems it should be monitored for. If your male cat suffers from chronic Feline Urological Syndrome (FUS), you should leave information to that effect and describe the warning signs of an onset of the problem. If your Dachshund has back problems, these should also be described, along with any treatments or precautions required. Note any allergies your pets have, including allergies to foods and medications. Note whether your pet is allergic to fleas or to flea-control products. Your vet can help you compile a history of pertinent information.

Your pet's guardian may not wish to or be able to use your regular veterinarian, but you should make sure that the guardian will be able to contact him for information if the need arises. If a complete record of your pet's medical history will be important for its future care, ask your veterinarian if he would be willing to transfer those records to a new veterinarian, or if he will provide copies to go into your file or to go directly to your pet's guardian after your death.

You should also make sure that your pet's vaccinations are current, and that this fact is documented in your pet's medical records. If your designated guardian needs to transport a pet across state lines, this can help avoid complications about undocumented vaccinations (and unnecessary veterinary costs to duplicate the vaccinations). Such a record can also be important if, for any reason, your pets must be temporarily impounded; it demonstrates that the pet is not liable to have any communicable diseases and that it is free of rabies.

6. Special instructions. If your pet has any quirks, preferences, dislikes, phobias, etc. that you believe its new owner should know about, write them down. For instance, if your dog takes a violent dislike to small children, you don't want its new owner to find out the hard way when her young nephew comes to visit for the first time. If your housecat is traumatized by thunderstorms and disappears for hours, you can save its new owner some stress by pointing out the habit.

Other things you may wish to call attention to include: special diets, special exercise needs, regular medications (such as heartworm preventive), old injuries that require a certain amount of consideration, items that your dog is most likely to destroy, the fact that your cat is declawed and should not be allowed outdoors, and so forth.

Kennel owners may have more specific instructions. In a kennel, certain dogs often form strong hate relationships; an executor or guardian needs to know which dogs should never be allowed together lest a major fight ensue.

7. Good homes. You may already know of people who might be willing to adopt your pets, though you plan to leave the actual placement arrangements to the guardian. It will help that person immensely if you prepare a list of such potential homes in advance and leave it with your papers. If certain people are likely to adopt specific pets, note this information. If breeders might be interested in specific animals, make sure your guardian has a list of appropriate breeders.

8. Funeral arrangements. If you have purchased cemetery plots for your pets, or have special wishes for the disposition of your pet's remains when it dies, specify these in your papers. For example, if you want your pet's ashes scattered on family property, make sure your guardian is aware of this. Most guardians will honor your wishes, but make sure that your requests are reasonable. If your pet is going to an excellent home across the country, it may not be feasible to have the pet transported back for a funeral. You might wish to state that existing cemetery reservations should be cashed in and used toward comparable arrangements elsewhere.

These records will be useful to your pets' guardian only if they are kept current. Update the information as it changes. Don't clutter the file with useless or confusing information; include only those items that will truly help your pets' guardian provide the best possible care or do the most effective job of placing your pets appropriately.

It's not pleasant to think about the possibility of one's own death. But it's even less pleasant to think about what could happen to your beloved pets if you haven't made provisions for them. If you haven't made arrangements for homes for your pets, they could wind up in animal shelters, adopted by uncaring owners, put to sleep, abandoned on the street or worse. In death as in life, it is the responsibility of a caring pet owner to provide for the animals we've chosen to bring into our lives.

Note: The information in this chapter is not intended to be a substitute for professional legal advice.

Chapter 10

Giving Up
A Pet

W E ALL WANT TO BELIEVE THAT, no matter what happens, we will be always be able to provide for and take care of our pets. Yet sometimes circumstances arise that make this impossible. When that happens, we face a decision that, in many respects, seems as painful as the decision to euthanize a pet: The need to find a new home for our animal companion.

Several types of situations can make it necessary for a person to give up a beloved pet. One of the most common is a move to a new home, perhaps in a location in which one either can't keep one's pets or can't provide them an environment in which they will be safe, comfortable, or happy. For example, a family that has to move from a rural or suburban environment to an urban area with less space, little or no yard, and (perhaps) intolerant neighbors, may find that it is kinder to seek a new home for its large, active dogs. So might a pet owner who is forced, for whatever reason, to move from a large house with a nice yard to a small, cramped apartment with no outdoor space. Sometimes a pet owner has no alternative but to move into housing that prohibits pets, or into an area that restricts the number or type of pets one may own.

Military families often face changes of station that make it impossible to keep the family pet. Sometimes it is simply not possible or affordable to transport the pet; in other cases, no housing will be available to accommodate the pet. A move to Hawaii involves a costly four-month quarantine, while a move to England requires an even costlier six-month quarantine. (It is important to note, however, that a move to continental Europe does not require a quarantine; we were surprised by the number of people who did not know this, and who assumed that when we made such a move, we would have to give up our cats. We didn't, and the cats had a fine time abroad. Wherever you go, check out the regulations and requirements first, and you may find that you can keep your pets after all!)

Changes within a family may also make it necessary to give up a pet. Divorce, death, marriage, the birth of a child, going back to work, gaining or losing a family member—all of these can affect your lifestyle, home environment, finances, and ability to take care of your pet. In the case of divorce, for example, one partner automatically "loses custody" of a pet— and the other may find it impossible to keep the pet as well. We knew a woman who moved to a small apartment after her divorce, and was finally forced to give up her dog because it barked all day while she was at work.

What happens if you marry someone who breaks out into hives or starts wheezing when your cat walks into the room? What if an older relative comes to live with you and has a similar reaction? What happens when your son goes off to college, leaving behind his extremely large and energetic dog? One woman gave up her cat after her baby was born because the cat, apparently jealous of the intruder, began to urinate throughout the house. Even "blended" pet-owning families can face problems: What happens when his Afghans don't get along with your Angoras?

Injuries and disabilities can strike any of us, no matter how healthy we are. Allergies, asthma, and other respiratory problems—all of which can be complicated by pet hair, pet "dander," and even the dirt pets can introduce into the home— are also common reasons for giving up pets.

Elderly pet owners, faced with health problems and increasing lack of mobility, are often forced to give up their pets, especially if they must move into a retirement or senior care facility. The problems of an elderly pet owner may be compounded by the fact that he has fewer contacts and resources to help him place the pet in a good home.

Whatever the reason for your decision, giving up a pet is something like a death and something like a divorce. While you can expect to feel all the pain and grief that you would experience if your pet had died, you may find it difficult to accept and work through that pain, because you know that your pet is still alive and—hopefully—healthy and happy. It's just somewhere else.

Counselor Diane Matheny writes, "The grieving process is similar enough to what we experience when a pet dies that we feel most of the same symptoms. When we give up a pet, however, it is sometimes hard to let ourselves grieve, because we rationalize too much. We think, 'I shouldn't feel this way because I know my pet isn't dead.' It's helpful to focus on the loss and what it means to your life, rather than on how the loss occurred. We still miss the pet terribly and feel guilty about our decisions, and need to take the same healing steps."

A Special Kind of Grief

When a pet dies, we often feel as though the circumstances involved were out of our control. We could not prevent the illness that claimed our pet's life, or the accident that snatched it from us. Even in the case of euthanasia, we often feel (correctly) that we have no other choice, that this is truly what is best for our beloved pet.

When we must decide to find a new home for a pet, however, the situation often does not seem so clear. We often feel responsible not only for the traumatic act of giving up the beloved pet, but for the circumstances that are causing us to make this decision.

For example, if you are moving because you or your spouse has changed or transferred jobs, and that move makes it necessary for you to find a new home for your pet, you may feel torn between two possible decisions. The new job may be what is best (or absolutely essential) for you and your family—but it also means giving up a family member that you love!

Such a situation can create a number of conflicting emotions, not only in you, but in every member of your family. Your children, instead of being happy about the family's good fortune, may be angry that your move (which they are less likely to understand) is causing the loss of their best friend. They may blame you for "forcing" them to part with a loved one, and be resentful of the move, the new job, and of you. In turn, you may be disappointed and even angry at your family's lack of enthusiasm and support—as well as upset about the loss that you face.

A change in the family structure can also create conflict. On the surface, you may suppose that it should be easy to choose between the needs of a human family member and a pet—but in reality, it is not so easy. You may realize that giving up a pet is necessary to protect the health of an allergic or asthmatic family member, but the fact remains that, in a very real sense, you are being asked to choose one loved one over another. It is easy to tell yourself that you "shouldn't" feel this way, that "of course humans come first," but the pain and resentment are still there.

You may feel guilty, thinking that you are an uncaring parent or family member because you find it so difficult to give up your pet, even for another's wellbeing. The fact is that you are not uncaring or selfish; you are simply a normal, loving human being who is being forced to make a deeply painful choice. Don't let anyone try to make you feel guilty, or convince you that the decision should be "easy."

When the allergic family member is a child, be prepared to handle the child's grief as well. A child who learns that the family pet—his personal furry friend—must go because of his health is likely to feel very guilty and resentful. It is hard enough for an adult to make this decision; it's a lot tougher for a child to feel responsible for the loss of his friend. Be sure to discuss this decision carefully with your child, and be careful what you say. Don't say "We have to get rid of Fido because he makes you sick." Instead, say something like "I know that you are going to miss Fido very much, but he loves you too much to want you to suffer, and he'll really be happier knowing that you are healthy." In such a situation, do everything you can to find Fido a good home; your child will feel even worse if he believes that Fido was sent to a shelter or perhaps euthanized because of his illness.

When you are the sick or injured one, you're likely to feel a great deal of guilt and anger. A person normally resents a sickness or injury that costs him mobility or the ability to function in the manner to which he is accustomed. When that illness or injury also means the loss of a beloved pet, one's resentment and anger are bound to be even stronger. If this should happen to you, you may feel as if you are weak, that you "should" be stronger, that you "should" be able to find a way to cope. You may be angry at the illness, at fate, at God— and in particular at yourself. In such a situation, accepting your anger and grief is important—but it is also important to work through your feelings, because they will only hinder your physical recovery.

Divorce or the death of a spouse or loved one carries its own burden of emotions—including grief, depression, anger, guilt, denial, and more. In such a situation, you are facing a double loss, and many people find that the loss of the pet is the proverbial "last straw." In some cases, this can actually be beneficial, as the loss of the pet may finally force a person to face the emotions that have been bottled up regarding the separation. In other cases, a person may focus upon the loss of the pet as a way to avoid dealing with other losses—which I have often found to be the situation when someone tells me that she has been grieving the loss of a pet for several years.

For an elderly pet owner, the decision to give up a pet— whether it is made by the owner or "forced" by external circumstances—can be especially painful. Often, a pet is an elderly person's only companion and friend, someone to talk to and receive unconditional affection from. For many, a pet is a last living reminder of bygone days and departed loved ones. Pets often give the elderly a reason for living.

When an elderly pet owner must give up a pet because of failing health or a move to a care facility, she faces not only the loss of this particular relationship and all it means, but the realization that her days as a pet owner are over. Many of us can look forward to having a new pet some day, even if we have to give up the pet we now own. Not so the elderly pet owner; he knows that there will never be another animal companion in his life, and this realization can be traumatic. If the pet has been an elderly person's primary companion and reason for living, he may feel as though he *has* no more reason for living; the loss of a pet may seem to represent "the beginning of the end."

"Giving up a pet is particular hard on the elderly," writes therapist Julie Janssen, M.D. "Often this is the last straw on the camel's back. The elderly have often lost so much already. They may have lost their status in society as wage earners and productive citizens. Many have lost close friends and relatives. Their physical abilities may be deteriorating, affecting their mobility and their feelings of independence. An elderly person may believe he or she is a nuisance or a bother to others. Having a companion animal is often one of the few ways in which an elderly person can feel helpful, needed, and loved."

Thus, in all situations, the process of giving up a pet involves not only the grieving processes described in previous chapters, but, quite often, a set of emotions and conflicts and traumas all its own. You may find it necessary to deal not only with your loss, but with issues involving the circumstances that are causing that loss to occur. It is often hard to separate these issues, to determine which emotions are related to the loss of your pet and which are related to the other situations in your life. It is important, however, to find ways to work through both; it can be tempting to avoid dealing with one trauma by focusing exclusively on another.

Family communication is especially important at a time like this. When a pet is ill or injured, your primary consideration is "what is best for my pet." When you are facing the decision to give up a pet, however, you must consider not only what is best for the pet but what is best for the whole family. Would it really help your family to rent a home that you cannot possibly afford, just to keep your dog? Would it really be in the best interest for your dog to keep it confined in a small apartment while you go to work all day? Will the trauma of losing a pet offset the health benefits?

Such decisions need to be discussed with all the family members involved, and the needs of everyone should be taken into consideration. Otherwise, when decisions are made in a vacuum or "arbitrarily," the anger and resentment of family members (especially children) can haunt you for years.

What Next?

Once you come to the decision, for whatever reason, that you must give up your pet, there are four important steps you can take to make this transition easier on you, your family, and your pet.

1. Plan ahead. Don't put off your decision until the last minute. It's tempting to keep hoping for a miracle that will make it possible for you to keep your pet—but the fact is, if that miracle is going to occur, it's more likely to be the result of diligent advance planning. Planning ahead will greatly reduce the pain experienced by you, your family, and your pet. It beats the agonizing uncertainty of having to send it to a shelter at the last minute!

2. Involve your family in the process. A pet is a family member, and its fate is a family affair. Everyone in the family needs to understand why this decision is being made, how it is being implemented, and how they can be involved. It may be tempting to withhold "the bad news" from your children until the last minute in the mistaken assumption that this spares them pain, but it never works. Instead, your children become victims of your decision—and you become a victim as well, because you end up having to bear the burden not only of your own pain and grief, but of your family's anger and resentment. Instead, make your children participants in the process, contributors to the future wellbeing of your pet.

Discussing the situation with your family gives you a chance to find out what everyone's feelings and priorities are. This is not the time to judge feelings or condemn them; let your family express their reactions, even if you don't appreciate their anger or resentment. Anger will only get worse if you refuse to listen to it, or tell people "not to feel that way."

This may also be a wonderful opportunity to discover and address potential problems in advance. For example, only by letting family members express themselves openly and honestly will you discover, perhaps, that your child is insecure about a move because she is leaving all her friends behind, which makes the loss of her pet even more traumatic.

Your family may offer alternatives that you wouldn't have

thought of. For example, if your children discover that you can't afford to move Fido, they may be willing to cut expenses or take on jobs to earn extra money. The farther in advance this process can begin, the more likely it is to work. Family members may be willing to pitch in to provide extra help with an unmanageable pet by working extra hard to keep the house clean or by taking the pet to obedience class.

Even if you can't work out a way to keep the pet, every family member has something to contribute. Encourage each member to work their personal "network" of friends, teachers, and coworkers. Perhaps your teenage son happens to know that his friend's dad just lost a dog, and would be interested in your adult pet. When family members perceive that they can contribute positively to the pet's future, they are less likely to react negatively to a situation over which, otherwise, they would feel they have no voice or control.

3. Network, network, network. If you have the advantage of time, use it! Make lists of possible owners. Discuss your problem with friends, relatives, neighbors, coworkers, acquaintances, and people you do business with. Use every office network available to you: e-mail, water-cooler gossip, bulletin boards. (My husband's workplace has an "animal lover's network" on e-mail, which has proven a great way to place strays.) Tell your pastor that you need a home for your pet; perhaps a notice can be placed in the church newsletter or on the bulletin board. Talk to carpool members. Mention it to your hairdresser, or any other person you do business with who might encounter other pet owners during the workday.

Check with all your relatives and close friends, especially those who care about pets. Don't overlook friends and relatives who live at a distance or in another state. If you can find a good home this way, it's worth the cost of shipping.

If you bought your pet from a breeder, the breeder may prefer you to return the pet so that he can find a suitable home for it. If you co-own a purebred pet, you may be able to return it to the co-owner. In either case, chances are good that the breeder or co-owner will be able to find your pet a home with someone who loves and understands the breed. You may also find help through a breed rescue society.

Network among your pet care professionals. Talk to your

veterinarian; if she knows your pet, she'll want to help you find it a good home. Talk to other veterinarians in town, as well as groomers and boarding kennels. Leave announcements in their offices. Some pet supply shops do not carry "puppies for sale," but serve as adoption centers for unwanted pets who need homes. These shops are dedicated to finding good, responsible homes for the pets they place. Talk to pet care professionals in person so that they will remember you, and be sure to bring a picture of your pet.

4. Explore other options in your area. Some cities have "no-kill" shelters that will keep a pet as long as necessary, until it is adopted or until it dies of old age. Some have permanent retirement communities of unadoptable or elderly pets. No-kill shelters are more common for cats than for dogs, but exist for both.

A shelter in the San Francisco Bay Area has instituted a program in which, whenever possible, pets available for adoption are not kept at the shelter, but remain in the home of their current owner. The shelter keeps a list of available pets, and sends prospective adopters to your home to meet you and your pet. This not only reduces the strain on the pet and on you, but gives you a chance to screen potential owners. Check with shelters in your area to see if they have such a program, or if they would be interested in handling your pet's adoption in a similar way.

Some towns have animal adoption newspapers in which you can list your pet. Some even have local TV or radio programs devoted to pet adoptions. And, of course, you can always advertise your pet in the local paper.

Should you advertise your pet as "free to good home"? Opinions differ on this issue. Some people believe that this is asking for trouble, citing horror stories of unscrupulous people who "adopt" free pets only to resell them, or worse, to sell them to research laboratories.

We've all heard these stories; like many gems of folk wisdom, they have been repeated endlessly by pet owners and others who, unfortunately, often have no real knowledge to back them up. That is not to say that such unscrupulous people do not exist, or that such tragedies have not occurred. I suspect, however, that they are not as common as the horror stories would lead us to believe—and you can take precautions to protect your pet from such a tragedy. If you are concerned about whether it is safe to advertise your pet, discuss the matter with your local animal control authorities; they will be able to advise you whether any such incidents have occurred or are suspected in your area.

Some people recommend that the best way to avoid unscrupulous adopters is to put a price on your pet, rather than advertising it as "free." They argue that, since a person must pay an adoption fee to an animal shelter or humane society, it is reasonable to place a similar "adoption fee" on your own pet. Proponents of this approach reason that a responsible pet owner should have no objection to paying from $25 to $100 for your pet, but that someone who is looking for a "free" pet may be unwilling to make the financial commitment that pet ownership involves.

Personally, I don't agree with this suggestion. When I see an ad that lists a pet as "free to good home," I assume that the owner's primary interest is, in fact, finding a good home for his pet. On the other hand, when I see a pet—a "previously owned pet," if you'll pardon the expression—being advertised for a price, even a low price, I begin to wonder. Is the owner looking for a home for his pet, or is he looking for money? For all I know, this might be the ad of one of those unscrupulous people mentioned above, who "adopt" free pets and resell them for a profit.

It is true that I would have no objection to paying a shelter's adoption fee—and I have. However, when I give my money to an animal shelter or humane organization, I know where it is going and why. I know my donation is being used to care for other abandoned and unwanted animals. Given the choice, I would far rather hand my money to a shelter than to an unknown individual who advertises a pet for sale in the paper.

To make sure that your pet actually does wind up in a good home, take steps to screen anyone who answers your ad. How does the person sound to you over the phone? Does he or she sound alert, reliable, knowledgeable about pets? Or does he avoid or evade your questions, contradict himself, or get angry when you ask about his approach to pet care?

Find out what the potential owner's attitudes are about

pet care, including diet, exercise, training, altering, indoor vs. outdoor pets, and so forth. Does the person regard the pet as a family member, or is she just looking for "a dog for the kids"? Who will be responsible for exercising the dog, or continuing its obedience training? Has the person owned pets before? Has the person owned this particular kind of pet? What does the person normally feed his pets—a nutritious pet food, or any off-the-shelf brand, or table scraps? Is the new owner interested in breeding your pet, and if so, why? Make sure the prospective owner believes in annual vaccinations; one neighbor of ours was convinced that "once was enough!"

Find out what happened to the person's previous pets, if any. Ask how long the person has been interested in obtaining a new pet; if the person says, "Oh, I just saw your ad and I thought it sounded like a neat idea," move on! You want to place your pet with someone who has given serious thought to pet ownership, not someone who wants to adopt a pet on impulse. Likewise, beware of a caller who says "I want to get a kitten for my girlfriend" or something similar!

A responsible pet owner should have no objection to answering these questions, provided you ask them nicely. In fact, a responsible pet owner might wonder about you if you *didn't* ask such questions. A good rule of thumb is to ask questions you wouldn't mind answering yourself. Make it a conversation, not an inquisition. If a person is reluctant to answer, is evasive, or seems offended by your questions, keep looking.

Once you have found a prospective owner who seems suitable, insist on meeting the person—the entire family, if possible—before you make a final decision. Ask to see the person's home and the facilities they have for the pet. Someone may sound like a wonderful prospective owner over the phone, but you will quickly change your mind if you visit the person's home and find that it is crawling with fleas, or that the person's "great yard" is actually a tiny patch of unshaded dirt.

On the other hand, if you discover that the prospective owner's home and family are all that you could have hoped for, the peace of mind this will give you as you hand over your pet will be a tremendous help in the grieving process that follows. You will be able to move on, knowing that you have truly made the best possible provision for your pet.

When the Day Comes

At last your research, networking, and planning have paid off. You have found a new home for your pet, and it's time to say good-bye. This is the day you have been dreading. How can you make it as painless as possible, or even a positive experience, for you, your family, and your pet?

First, resist the temptation to start "second-guessing" your decision. When the day comes to actually part with your pet, all the emotions you have been holding in check are likely to hit you at once. You knew, intellectually, that this was going to hurt—but now the pain is hitting you at a gut level, and it may seem more than you can bear. It can be very tempting to change your mind—but it is rarely a good idea.

This is not the time to start agonizing over all the things you think you might have, could have, or should have done, or done differently. Nor is it the time to wonder if you should have pursued different options, made different choices, or "tried harder." Your decision has been made; the best thing you can do now, for yourself, your family, and your pet is to follow through and accept that you have done the best you could. Keep this in mind, too, when other family members—who are also suddenly experiencing the reality of grief—become more vocal in their anger or resentment.

If possible, involve every family member in the departure. Everyone will feel a need to say a final good-bye to the pet, so be sure that you allow each family member a chance to make a personal, private farewell. On the final day, you may find that one of your children doesn't want to participate, preferring to sulk in her room with the door shut. This is understandable, but encourage the child to say good-bye; later, she is likely to feel even guiltier for not having said farewell, and may fear that the pet will think she didn't love it.

The process of saying a formal good-bye to the pet provides every family with a point of separation. The decision has been made, the time has come, and the reality of the loss has struck home. This may be a time when you can cry together, grieve together, hug and comfort one another, and face the pain as a united family. It is not a time to scold someone for tears, get upset if a family member reacts with an outburst of anger, or insist that everyone "put on a happy face" or "stop acting upset." Don't be surprised if a family member reacts negatively to the pet's new owner; he may feel as if that person is "stealing" the pet, or trying to replace him in the pet's affections. Don't tell your children to be strong and not cry, and don't pretend that you shouldn't feel bad because everything is really for the best. You will feel bad, all of you, and the best way to resolve your feelings is to let them happen and accept them. Otherwise, grief and anger and resentment may simmer under the surface for a long time to come.

Consider holding some sort of farewell ceremony for the pet. One possibility is a party the night before, featuring the pet's favorite foods and treats (such as a tuna or hamburger cake), and special gifts for the pet to take to its new home. Again, this may be a time of tears and pain, as well as shared memories, but it can be a valuable way to ease the parting.

Counselor Diane Matheny writes, "Saying good-bye is the hardest part of all, but I feel it is important for the current owner to make the gesture of giving the animal to the new owner. The animal can see and hear how you speak to the new family, and I believe this can transmit confidence to it that this is not a threatening situation. It is also a 'finishing' gesture, much like saying good-bye when a pet is euthanized. It is a time to say anything we need to say and to thank the pet for having been a part of our lives. It is very difficult, but prevents regrets over not having told them how we feel."

Gather together your pet's favorite things: its dish, blanket or bed, toys, collar, etc. You will be happier knowing that your pet still has its favorite possessions, and it will appreciate having familiar things in its new home. You might also want to throw in an old shirt or other item of clothing to give the pet something with a familiar scent; this can help it adjust to its new environment.

Be sure to pass along all the important papers and information associated with your pet. Make up a packet that includes the following:

• Your pet's "vital statistics": Name (including kennel name and call name, if appropriate), age, sex, and whether or not it is altered.

• Pedigrees and AKC or other registration.

• Show history, breeding history, and any other information that the new owner will need if he is interested in continuing your pet's show career. (If you have a handler, you might want to provide that person's name to the new owner.)

• Local licenses and registration.

• Medical records, including vaccination certificates. Also include the name and number of your veterinarian, so that the new owner can contact her with any questions about the pet's health or medical history. Be sure to include any information about important health conditions, allergies, or necessary medications.

• The names of any pet care professionals who might be helpful to the new owner, such as the breeder from whom you bought the pet, the pet's trainer, groomer, and so forth.

• Funeral arrangements, if any. (Remember, however, that the pet's new owner is under no obligation to honor the arrangements you have already made; if you have already reserved a cemetery plot for your pet, you might wish to cash it in if the owner is not interested in using it.)

• Special instructions, including information about the pet's diet, exercise needs, quirks, phobias, habits, training background, and special commands (don't let the new owner find out by accident, for example, that you've trained your Doberman to attack on the word "Down"!). If your dog has a tendency to snap at children or attack other pets, make sure the new owner knows this in advance—or, among other complications, you could face a lawsuit! Make sure the owner knows that your cat is declawed and shouldn't be let outside, that your Dachshund shouldn't be allowed to climb stairs because of a strained back, or that your arthritic Poodle needs a sweater in cold weather. Keep in mind, however, that this list should be confined to *important* instructions; if you have been in the habit of feeding your pet fresh liver and reading it poetry every night before bed (I am not making this up!), don't expect the new owner to be enthusiastic about continuing the practice.

One way to have your children participate in the process is to ask each of them to write a personal letter to the new owner, describing the things they consider especially important for the owner to know about the pet. Such letters help your children feel that they are making a positive contribution to their beloved pet's future, and are likely to be treasured by the new owner as well.

After you have handed your pet over to its new owner, resist the temptation to visit—at least not more than once. Some people suggest that you arrange for one follow-up visit to make sure that everything is working out for both the pet and the new owner, but if all is going well, that should be the end of it. Be available for calls and questions, but don't keep calling the new owner "just to find out how Fido is doing," and stay away. Visiting your pet in its new home makes it harder for you to adjust to your loss, and for your pet to adapt to its life without you. It can also send the wrong message to the new owner, implying that you are "checking up" and don't trust the owner to take proper care of your pet. Your pet has moved on—and so must you.

Chapter 11

Helping
A Friend

I MENTIONED IN EARLIER CHAPTERS that this book would not be a miracle cure that magically banishes grief overnight. So it seemed logical to round off the last chapter with some additional comforting reminders that you will be able to work through your grief and return to a normal life and that you will be able to love and enjoy new pets while keeping fond memories of departed friends. But I've already said all these things.

Then a package came from Jean-Irene U. of Illinois that brought the final chapter into focus. Jean, it seemed, wasn't content to work through her own grief and get on with life; she wanted to help other pet owners as well. Her particular method was to make condolence cards for friends whose pets had died; since her hobby was photography, she designed each card around a photo of the departed pet.

That attitude seems to me the best possible result of coming to terms with pet loss. If you, as a pet owner, can use the information in this book to get your own life back on an even keel, that's wonderful. If you can use it to help a friend or relative who is suffering the pain and loss you have suffered, that is wonderful beyond words. You'll have turned your experience, harsh as it was, into a positive source of support and caring for others. Now that you have a framework for handling grief, you can pass that framework on, and be the understanding friend that so many pet owners have looked for in vain.

The support of friends can make a tremendous difference to a grieving pet owner, as you may have already discovered. "Some understanding people made what could have been an unbearable ordeal livable," wrote Jacqueline R. of New York. Joyce W. of Delaware wrote, "My family was sorry about my Doberman's death, but not very supportive. But I had a dear friend who came over and sat with me for one full afternoon, and we talked and cried together about Cinni. This friend knew what I was suffering. She lost her old dog two years before. Believe me, it helped, just knowing someone else cared and knew how much Cinni meant to me."

"Our next-door neighbor came over and stayed with me," wrote Celia P. of New York. "We had a pot of tea and talked about Cammie's life. She was wonderful. Some people couldn't understand why I was so upset over 'just a dog,' but others were fantastic. We got sympathy cards and letters, and the phone was ringing off the hook. People had loved that little guy, and they acted just as they would have for a human family member."

"My sister was willing to spend the night, and one friend came right over," wrote Karen A. of Illinois. "My entire family and a few friends came over the next day. A true family member had died. I had some help the next day in bringing his body to the vet for disposal. I never would have imagined the outpouring of sympathy and understanding. They knew my hurt, never made me feel silly—it was so wonderful."

"I recommend that people send sympathy cards or notes to the grieving pet owner," said Cathy W. of California. "It really helped me to know that people cared enough about Shelly to take time to write. Also, our veterinarian sent a note. I'm a groomer, and when one of my clients' babies dies, I always call or write. It seems to help, talking to someone who cared about your baby."

Other pet owners have found that the experience has helped them deal with the losses encountered by others. "Until I experienced this, I did not understand what people went through with the death of a pet," wrote Jan R. of Tennessee. "I was not sympathetic toward others, but now I am and am able to talk to other people who are going through this."

Sharon H. of Indiana found that the loss of her pet helped prepare her for the later loss of a human family member: "Less than a week after we lost Lucy, my father-in-law had a heart attack. I will say the loss of my pets prepared me to deal with his death much better. I knew the kind of feelings I would be having and that sometimes you have to let go of the one you love because you do love them and want them to suffer no more. I was able to help my husband and his family deal with their grief. I have come to believe that things do happen for a reason, and that the hardest lessons are the ones we benefit from the most."

Ten Tips for Helping Others

1. Just being there and being supportive is the best help anyone can provide. Many pet owners find themselves surrounded by people who don't understand, who make "it was just an animal" comments and, without meaning to, make a grieving pet owner feel much worse. Even one person like yourself who can say, "I know what you're going through; I've been there myself; Fido was a wonderful dog, wasn't he?" can make the difference.

2. Encourage your friend or relative to express his or her grief. People are often ashamed to cry in front of others, even in front of relatives or close friends. To compound the problem, many people are embarrassed or made uncomfortable by a display of emotion, and may make comments that are intended to cause the grieving person to "buck up" but may actually cause additional pain.

If you think your friend's tears will embarrass you, remember how you felt when you suffered a loss. Remember that what is important now is what will help your friend cope. You may find, too, that as you encourage your friend to open up, your own heart opens as well, and your embarrassment or discomfort disappears. Never, never do or say anything that will make your friend feel silly for his emotions; again, remember how you felt.

You may find that your friend's experience brings back painful memories of your own. When our family visited one Christmas, an incident reminded my mother-in-law of her cat, who had died a few months before, and she began to cry. I found myself crying right along with her. There's nothing wrong with a group cry; if the painful emotions still exist within you, it's healthier to express them than to repress them.

3. Act as a buffer, taking on some of your friend's burden. If the friend must take a pet to be euthanized, offer to accompany her to the vet. Offer to drive, so that your friend can spend some last moments in the car with the pet—and while you're driving, stay out of the farewells and keep your eyes on the road. Ask if your friend would like you to go into the vet's office with her, but don't push if the answer is no. On the way home, let your friend choose whether or not she wants to talk, or just to sit silently and think or cry.

You may be able to help by taking the pet's body to the vet, or to a cemetery or crematorium. If you haven't had the experience of touching or handling a dead animal, you might think this sounds unpleasant. You will be surprised to find that there's nothing creepy or gross about picking up the body of an animal that you've loved and hugged all its life; its fur is still soft, and you may find yourself wanting to give it one more good-bye cuddle before taking it to its final destination.

You can offer your help in making funeral arrangements, too. If your friend wishes to have his pet buried at a cemetery, you can gather information or make arrangements; your friend may find this difficult to do without breaking down. If your friend has already made plans for the disposal of his pet, you can notify the cemetery or crematorium of the pet's arrival, or arrange to have it picked up.

4. Make yourself available after the immediate period of death. Many people are full of condolences when a family member dies, but after a few days they seem to disappear. Yet the period beginning a few days after the initial loss, after the shock and numbness have worn off, can be the hardest on a bereaved pet owner. This is when the pet owner begins to realize how much he has lost, how much the pet meant, and how empty the days will be without the pet. He will find it difficult to establish new routines, because so much of the

pattern of his life was based around caring for and interacting with the pet. During this period it's easy for a pet owner to get trapped in a cycle of depression and inactivity.

Make an effort to get your friend involved in other activities in the days and weeks that follow the death of the pet. Make arrangements to go to a movie, or to some event that you both can enjoy and that will be a distraction. Go shopping together. Or just visit, sharing tea or coffee (why not bring along a cake or some cookies?) and memories.

Exercise your best judgment as to whether you should involve your friend in anything that will remind him of the lost pet. For some, turning this period of mourning into a period of helping other homeless animals is helpful; others find even the sight of another animal too painful to bear.

5. Share any insights you have gained on coping with grief. If you've learned a particularly helpful coping strategy from this book, or from any other source, pass it along. But remember that every person is unique, and what worked well for you may not work well for someone else. If your first suggestion isn't well received, look for an alternative rather than pressing the point. Keep in mind that your friend's situation and needs may be different from your own.

6. Send your friend a condolence card. Several companies manufacture condolence cards for pets. Or, you can design your own, like Jean-Irene does. The card doesn't have to be elaborate, and you don't need to think up highly creative expressions of sympathy; the gesture is what counts.

7. Make a donation in the pet's name to an appropriate charity. Organizations such as the Morris Animal Foundation (which researches cures for various animal diseases), many SPCAs and humane societies, animal sanctuaries and more are supported almost entirely by charitable donations. One pet owner wrote that her mother had sent a donation to a local wolf sanctuary, and had donated every year since then to commemorate the deceased pet's birthday. In most cases the organization you donate to will send a card to the pet owner acknowledging the donation, without revealing the amount, in the name of the pet. Check around in your area for organizations that will accept or can process memorial donations, or ask your veterinarian for his suggestions.

8. Share your pet, if your friend seems to desire the company of another animal. Some pet owners find that having a visit from a cat or dog that they can love and hug, but that they don't have to make an emotional commitment to just yet, is very therapeutic. You might want to say something like, "Fifi wants to come over and say hello to Aunt Margaret," and see how your friend reacts to the idea. Be aware that some pet owners don't want to see another pet at this time, for it only reminds them of their loss. Again, base your decision on your knowledge of your friend's personality.

9. If you think it will be well-received, use a special talent of your own to make a memorial for the friend. My gift to my in-laws was a needlepoint portrait of their cat, which I began when I learned the cat did not have much longer to live. If you have pictures of the pet, consider getting one enlarged and frame it. If you are an artist, consider making a sketch of the pet, perhaps from an existing photo. If you enjoy writing, write a eulogy or a poem, and print it in calligraphy or a nice font on pretty paper, and frame that for your friend. A combination of a poem and a picture can be effective; if you aren't a poet yourself, find a published poem that seems to express the pet's nature or the joy of a pet/owner relationship, and include it with a picture of the pet.

10. If you're the supervisor of a pet owner who has just lost a pet, be understanding. Give your employee a day off if he or she needs to grieve privately. Don't be surprised if that person's work-flow slows up for a day or two; it's very difficult to concentrate when grieving. The employee will work twice as hard in a few days to get caught up again, and will appreciate your consideration. If you hear comments from the employee's coworkers that indicate a lack of understanding of the situation, point out without going into unnecessary detail that the employee is going through a very difficult time, and that the coworkers' understanding will be appreciated.

Some Pitfalls to Avoid

Sometimes a well-meaning friend can do something by accident that does more harm than good. Here's a list of "don'ts" that can help you avoid potentially harmful actions.

1. *Don't* rush out and buy your friend a new pet, thinking

that this will take his or her mind off the loss. Many people react with resentment and even hatred toward an "intruder" that is introduced too early into the household. A person who has lost a beloved pet needs time to accept that loss and make his own decision about when the time is right for a new pet. If one is brought in too early, the pet can suffer for being resented, rejected and unloved; the friend may try to keep the pet just so to avoid hurting your feelings, and end up with an animal that will never be fully accepted into the household. Worse, the pet may end up at an animal shelter and be put to sleep because the friend just can't handle it at this time.

In addition, the selection of a pet is a personal one, not one that should be made for someone else. If you know that your friend would someday like to have another dog or cat, and you would like to give the pet to your friend, give a "coupon" for the pet instead. Promise the friend that when he feels the time is right, the two of you will go to a pet shop or breeder or shelter, and you will pay for the pet he picks out. But don't rush your friend into a hasty choice.

2. *Don't* judge or criticize anything your friend did during the pet's last illness or death. Regardless of your personal feelings, avoid statements such as "you should have been there when it was put to sleep" or "you should have gotten a second opinion" or "you should have had it put to sleep weeks ago." These statements may be true, but what's done is done; you can't change the past. All this does is add an extra dose of guilt to the pain your friend is already feeling.

By the same reasoning, don't tell your friend what *you* would have done in her situation, or what you wouldn't have done, or what you think she should have done. If, for example, your friend gave up a pet, don't remark that you could never have done such a thing; this implies that, somehow, your friend is less caring than you. Support your friend's grief even if you don't agree with her decisions.

Instead, if your friend begins to say that the death was his fault, that he should have done this or should not have done that, try gently to defuse the situation. Emphasize all the good things he did for the pet while it was alive. The time to give counsel is before an action is taken—you may, for instance, be able to give advice on the handling of the next pet.

3. *Don't* try to force your friend into any actions he is not ready for. I mentioned distracting your friend with activities earlier in this chapter; if, however, your friend steadfastly refuses to leave the house, come over to your place for dinner, etc., don't push it. You can offer help, but you can't force someone to accept it; that door has to open from inside.

4. *Don't* be insulted if your friend doesn't want to come anywhere near your happy, bouncy, living pet. To some, this is an all-too-painful reminder of loss. Your friend isn't rejecting you or your pet; he is simply avoiding additional pain. As time goes on, this attitude will probably change.

5. *Don't* dismiss your friend's pain with glib statements such as "time heals all wounds" or "you'll get another pet." As we've seen from previous chapters, in essence these statements are true. Most pet owners recover from their grief and go on to love other pets. But at a time of grief, such statements seem callous and trite, and serve no purpose. Instead, let your friend lead the conversation with statements of his feelings and desires, and express your understanding of those feelings.

6. *Don't* regale your friend with horror stories. If your friend's pet is dying of cancer or must be euthanized soon, don't choose this time to tell the friend about something awful you've heard about the disease, or dreadful rumors about inhumane euthanasia practices. Chances are that the latter are untrue; bad rumors spread a lot faster and a lot less accurately than good ones. Avoid any discussions that will make your friend feel worse, or more uncertain, about the course of action he is choosing.

By the same token, don't share horror stories of what happened to your own pets. If your friend's dog is dying of liver failure, a gruesome account of how your dog suffered through the same thing isn't going to help. Instead, supply constructive advice: "Yes, I've heard that is a very serious problem and, really, euthanasia is the kindest thing you can do for the animal—but believe me, I know how tough it is!"

7. *Don't* let yourself become involved in family arguments. If the death of the pet, euthanasia, or the question of whether or not the family should get a new pet is causing friction, do your best to stay out of it. Sometimes, wittingly or unwittingly, a pet owner will use your support as a weapon to give

strength to his side of the argument. "Sally says we should do thus-and-so" is a good way to make you, Sally, unappreciated by family members with opposing views, and make you unwelcome in the household. If you sense that the loss of a pet is creating stress on family relationships, step back and lend your support from afar, with sympathy cards or donations. Let your friend know that you understand and are willing to help, but don't contribute to conversations that end up condemning other family members. If the situation is truly bad, suggest counseling.

8. Finally, *don't* give up on a friend who seems to be reacting differently from the way you reacted, or whose grief is lasting longer than yours did. If your friend is trying to put a brave face on things, denying that she is feeling any pain, you might try to draw her out with a statement about how you cried for three days when your dog died, how you thought the world had come to an end, or whatever other feelings you suspect your friend is concealing. Your friend simply may not be aware that there are people like you who find grief over pet loss acceptable. Sometimes it takes time to break through. And if you recovered in a few weeks but your friend's grief is dragging on for months, remember that the friend's relationship may have been different from yours. Don't measure everyone's experience by your own yardstick.

Love and friendship are what pets are all about. Sometimes we learn our first lessons of love and caring from pets; these may be the best friends we had in childhood, the most faithful friends we had as adults. The ideal extension of that relationship is to spread that love and friendship outward, to other pet owners (and even non-pet owners) who need it. You may also find, if you are still in the grieving process, that the best way to heal yourself is to reach out to heal someone else. As you ease someone else's pain, cry for another's loss, and rebuild both lives together, you may well wake up one day to find that you have passed through your own misery and come out a stronger, more understanding person for it. It's just one more amazing benefit pets bring to our lives.

Additional Resources

Looking for More Help?

Bereavement Counseling

To find a bereavement counselor in your area who deals with pet loss issues, first check with:

- Your veterinarian, and other local veterinarians.
- Local shelters (many offer support groups and other counseling services).
- The veterinary teaching department of a college or university in your region or state (many have pet loss support hotlines as well as counseling facilities).
- The yellow pages (many counselors and therapists now advertise this specific expertise).
- The hospice or counseling department of a hospital.
- The counseling ministry or pastoral care department of a local church (churches often host external, non-religious support groups, including pet loss groups).
- Counseling advertisements in a local animal-related newspaper (usually available for free through veterinarians and pet supply stores).

Note: A listing in this section does not constitute an explicit recommendation of the product or service on the part of the author or the publisher.

Directories of Counselors & Support Groups

The annual *Directory of Pet Loss Resources* lists nearly 70 counselors nationwide, and is available for $3 from:

    The Delta Society
    289 Perimeter Rd. East
    Renton, WA 98055-1329
    (206) 226-7357

The *Pet Loss Foundation* offers a database of counselors, pet loss support groups, hotlines, pet cemeteries, pet burial products (such as urns and caskets), books, and other resources throughout the U.S. To locate a counselor or other service in your area, write to:

    The Pet Loss Foundation
    1312 French Rd., Suite A-23
    Depew, NY 14043

The 1996 National Directory of Bereavement Support Groups and Services lists pet loss support groups and counselors as well as general bereavement support groups and resources. The 496-page directory is available for $29.95 plus $4 s/h from:

    ADM Publishing
    P.O. Box 751155
    Forest Hills, NY 11375-8755
    (718) 657-1277; fax (718) 297-6117

Pet Loss Bereavement Hot Lines:

National: Grief Recovery Hotline, (800) 445-4808
Mon-Fri 9 am-5 pm (Pacific Time)

Arizona: (602) 995-5885
24-hour hotline

Companion Animal Association of Arizona
P.O. Box 5006
Scottsdale, AZ 85261-5006

California: (916) 752-4200
Mon-Fri 6:30 pm - 9:30 pm (Pacific Time)

Pet Loss Support Hotline
Bonnie Madur, Assoc. Director
School of Veterinary Medicine
University of California
Davis, CA 95616

Florida: (904) 392-4700 ext. 4080

College of Veterinary Medicine
University of Florida
2015 SW 16th Ave.
Gainesville, FL 32610-0125

Massachusetts: (508) 839-7966
T/Th 6-9 pm (Eastern Time)

Tufts University
School of Veterinary Medicine
200 Westboro Rd.
N. Grafton, MA 01536

Michigan: (517) 336-2696
T/Th 7:30-9:30 pm (Eastern Time)

Pet Loss Support Hotline
College of Veterinary Medicine
Michigan State University, G100
East Lansing, MI 48824

Texas: (210) 227-4357
Daily 7 am - 3 am (Central Time)

United Way Helpline
P.O. Box 898
San Antonio, TX 78293

Additional Sources of Telephone Counseling

Colorado State University
School of Veterinary Medicine (Ft. Collins)
(303) 221-4535

Chicago Veterinary Medical Association
(708) 603-3994

(Calls to Chicago VMA may be placed any time, and will be returned 7-9 pm Central Time; long-distance calls will be returned collect.)

University of Minnesota
School of Veterinary Medicine (St. Paul)
(612) 624-4747

The Animal Medical Center
New York City, New York
(212) 838-8100

University of Pennsylvania
School of Veterinary Medicine (Philadelphia)
(215) 898-4525

Pet Loss Partnership
Washington State University
College of Veterinary Medicine (Pullman)
(509) 335-4569

In addition to these listings, many counselors also provide telephone counseling, some at no charge.

Support Resources in Canada

Pet Loss Support Group
12 Eaton Ave.
Dartsmouth, Nova Scotia B2Y 2X5
(902) 479-2869

Pet Loss Support Group of Calgary
c/o Patricia Frank
1234 8th St. SW
Calgary, Alberta T2R 1A9
(403) 248-6613

Pet Cemetery Information:

The Accredited Pet Cemeteries Society
139 W. Rush Rd.
W. Rush, NY 14543
(716) 533-1685

International Association of Pet Cemeteries
Rt. 11, Box 163
Ellensburg Depot, NY 12935
(518) 594-3000

Pet Caskets, Headstones, Urns, and Memorials

Many manufacturers of pet memorial products list their services in the classified sections of the major pet magazines, including *Dog Fancy, Cat Fancy, Dog World, Cats,* and *Purebred Dogs / The AKC Gazette.* In addition, several such manufacturers now feature home pages on the Internet.

Identification Registry Information

National Dog Registry
P.O. Box 166
Woodstock, NY 12498
(800) NDR-DOGS

TATOO-A-PET
1625 Emmons Ave.
Brooklyn, NY 11235
(800) TATTOOS

AKC Companion Animal Recovery
5580 Centerview Dr.
Raleigh, NC 27606-3394
(919) 233-9767; fax (919) 233-1290

(Registers microchip identification.)

Purebred Rescue Groups:

1. Check with a national or regional breed club for information about rescues. A local breeder may be able to provide you with the addresses of national and regional clubs.

2. *Dog Fancy* publishes an annually updated directory of national purebred clubs. For a copy of the list, write:

> Dog Fancy
> P.O. Box 6050
> Mission Viejo, CA 92690
> (714) 855-8822

3. *Project BREED Directory*, an annual directory of rescue organizations, can be obtained from Project BREED Inc. Call or write to the address below to locate a specific rescue, or for current directory price information. (Calls will be returned collect.)

> Project BREED Inc.
> P.O. Box 15888
> Chevy Chase, MD 20852-5888
> (202) 244-0065

Online Resources for Pet Loss Bereavement

This list reflects the resources on pet loss readily available on the Internet as of July 1996. However, new sites are being added to the World Wide Web almost daily. As sites are added, many of these home pages will add new links to help you navigate the net. Searching for "pet loss" via a net search program may help you discover additional resources. Unless otherwise noted, these listings are accessible through Netscape.

• **Alt.support.grief.pet-loss** — A newsgroup for on-line correspondence, discussion, and support.

• **http://catless.ncl.ac.uk/VMG** — The "Virtual Memorial Garden," features tributes, poems, memorials, etc. (Accessible through Mosaic but not through Netscape.)

• **http://rivendell.org/index.html** — GriefNet home page, with links to general bereavement sources. Also sponsors an on-line pet loss support group (majordomo@falcon.ic.net).

• **http://seniors-site.com/pets/pethotln.html** — Provides information from the U.C. Davis hotline, and links to other resources. (Accessible through Mosaic but not Netscape.)

• **http://www.cowpoke.com/~twscan/Pet.html** — A pet loss/bereavement home page with a number of links to other pages (including those listed below) and grief resources.

• **http://www.cowpoke.com/~twscan/NWPM/Grief.html** — A text page on dealing with grief.

• **http://www.lavamind.com/pet.html** — A"Virtual Pet Cemetery," where participants can post tributes to departed pets. (For information, E-mail pet.sponsor@lavamind.com).

• **http://www.microserve.net/~dave/bereave.htm** — A collection of comforting poems celebrating pets.

• **http://www.netwalk.com/~copydoc/pet-loss.htm** — The "Lightning Strike" home page, which "offers a 'cybershoulder' for grieving pet owners." Links to a variety of pet and pet loss resources (including those listed here).

• **http://ourworld.compuserve.com/homepages/edwilliams/** — Links to the "Rainbow Bridge" and Monday Candle Ceremony pages, and provides pages in which pet's name can be added to tribute lists, departed lists, and a "needs" list. Names will also appear on Prodigy, CompuServe, AOL, and GEnie.

• **http://www.primenet.com/~meggie/petloss.htm** — Offers text on coping with pet loss, as well as links to other pet-loss sites and useful references.

• **http://www.primnet.com/~meggie/bridge.htm** — "Remembrance" pages feature poems, photos, and tributes to departed pets; your tribute can be listed here as well.

• **http://www.primnet.com/~meggie/brdg.link.htm** — Links to the "Rainbow Bridge" page, which includes poetry and a guide to the on-line "Monday Candle Ceremony."

• **http://www.rahal.net/hredlus/pet-loss.htm/references** — A helpful list of pet loss references.

• **http://www2.pcix.com/~laytin/yankee/coping.htm** — A text page on dealing with grief.

America On-Line:
  Animals & Society Forum

Pet Care
Pet Care Message Center

CompuServe:
Pet Products Forum (see "Delta/Pet Books")
GO TWPETS (see "Saying Goodbye")

Prodigy:
Pets BB
Pets To Heaven

About the Author

Moira Anderson says, "On a typical day (like right now) you'll find me defending my keyboard and chair against two cats, who can't understand why I sometimes seem to think that writing is more important than petting. They may have a point..." Nevertheless, Anderson has been writing steadily since 1979, and has published three books ("three and a half if you count this second edition") and numerous articles. She is a member of the Dog Writer's Assocation of America, and was editor of the magazine *Dog Fancy* between 1985 and 1987. Anderson, who holds an M.Ed. in counseling from Boston University, teaches writing at St. Martin's College and is currently working on a novel.

Would you like to help a friend?

If you have a friend or loved one who's grieving over the loss of a pet, *Coping with Sorrow on the Loss of Your Pet* makes a wonderful, caring gift. Ask for a copy in your local bookstore, or order directly from:

Alpine Publications
P O Box 7027, Loveland, CO 80537

Additional Titles of Interest:

How to Raise a Puppy You Can Live With
Rutherford and Neil
This book is a "must" for every breeder, as well as for
new puppy owners!

It's A Dog's Life Pet Diary
Newman
Get this for your new puppy. It's like a baby book for keeping all his
memories.

Living with Small and Toy Dogs
Jester
All about the small breeds, from terrier to toy, and how to train,
relate to, and enjoy them.

Owner's Guide to Better Behavior in Dogs
Campbell
The best book on preventing or changing problem behavior, how
dog's think, and why they do what they do. Gentle, humane, works
with every dog.

Positively Obedient: Good Manners for the Family Dog
Handler
Train your dog to be well behaved and perform simple commands
like Sit and Down without learning all the precise exercises required
if you want to show in obedience. Humane, easy lessons
for the famiy dog.

For a Free Catalog of Alpine Books
please write to our Customer Service Department,
or call toll free 1-800-777-7257.